7/96 - 5 (3)

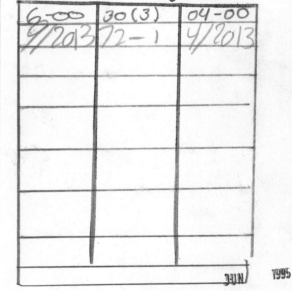

Collection Management

6-00	30 (3)	04-00
9/2013	72-1	4/2013

JUN 1995

Marco Polo

THE WORLD'S GREAT EXPLORERS

Marco Polo

By Zachary Kent

CHILDRENS PRESS ®

CHICAGO

Medallions of Marco Polo and Kublai Khan

Project Editor: Ann Heinrichs
Designer: Lindaanne Donohoe
Cover Art: Steven Gaston Dobson
Engraver: Liberty Photoengraving

j910.92
P778
<87

**Library of Congress
Cataloging-in-Publication Data**

Kent, Zachary
  Marco Polo / by Zachary Kent.
    p.   cm. — (The World's great explorers)
  Includes bibliographical references and index.
  Summary: Describes the travels of the medieval
Italian explorer and his adventures and discover-
ies in the Far East.
  ISBN 0-516-03070-1
  1. Polo, Marco, 1254-1323?—Journeys—Juvenile
literature. 2. Voyages and travel—Juvenile
literature. 3. Explorers—Italy—Biography—
Juvenile literature. 4. China—Description and
travel—to 1900—Juvenile literature. [1. Polo,
Marco, 1254-1323? 2. Explorers. 3. Voyages and
travels.] I. Title. II. Series.

                                    91-34521
G370.P9K46 1992   CIP
915.04'2—dc20   AC

Marco Polo's expedition leaving Venice for China, from a fourteenth-century manuscript in the Bodleian Library, Oxford, England

Table of Contents

Chapter 1
A Description of the World

Blaring trumpets brought people rushing to the Genoa waterfront on an autumn day in 1298. Messengers hurried through the crowd spreading exciting news. For years war had raged between the rival Italian city-states of Genoa and Venice. Now the Genoese learned they had scored a great victory over their enemy at the sea battle of Curzola.

Gazing across the harbor, the people soon wildly cheered. Genoese warships towed the defeated Venetian fleet toward the shore. In disgrace the captured galleys were pulled along backwards, their banners dragging in the water. Before long, seven thousand Venetian sailors shuffled along the docks on their way to dungeon cells. Among these prisoners walked forty-four-year-old Marco Polo. Marco Polo was the commander of one of the captured galleys and a Venetian gentleman. Instead of a common jail, therefore, the Genoese locked him in a tower of the Palace San Giorgio.

Many other prisoners shared these cramped quarters. Some men sat against the walls cursing their fate. Others paced back and forth in boredom. Still others told stories of their lives to fill the time. After a while Marco Polo was invited to tell some of his own experiences. The prisoners gathered around as Marco Polo began describing his travels. The tales that poured from his mouth were more fantastic than any the men had ever heard before. This Marco Polo claimed that for twenty-five years he had journeyed back and forth across faraway Asia. He described long sea voyages and desert caravans, fearsome Mongol armies, and glittering Chinese palaces.

Marco Polo's cellmates refused to let him stop, and he was pleased to have an audience. Day after day he continued spinning tales of his fabulous adventures. The prisoners gaped with wonder to learn of foreign princesses and magical wizards, strange customs, and frightening wild beasts. Even the jailors listened closely at the door, hardly believing their ears. Soon word of Marco Polo and his amazing stories spread throughout Genoa. Important Genoese citizens sometimes entered the cell to hear the stories for themselves.

Among the prisoners in the Palace San Giorgio was a man from Pisa named Rustichello. Captured during a battle between Pisa and Genoa, Rustichello already had spent over a dozen years in prison. He listened to the tales of Marco Polo with special interest. Before his imprisonment, Rustichello had gained some success as a writer of medieval romances. In the popular writing style of the day, his books recounted tales of noble heroes who killed giants and rescued fair maidens. His best known book was a telling of the legend of King Arthur and the knights of the Round Table.

"Dragons" of China, from a volume of the Travels of Marco Polo

Marco Polo's stories greatly impressed Rustichello. Here was a real hero. He had crossed mysterious lands and had sailed unknown seas. His life was full of adventures and he had traveled to the end of the world. Quickly Rustichello offered to set the Venetian traveler's stories down in writing, and happily Marco Polo accepted.

The Genoese jailors willingly brought quill pens, inkpots, and parchment paper. Curiously they allowed Marco Polo to send to his father in Venice for notes he had kept during his journeys. With his notes in hand to help his memory, Marco Polo began again the telling of his tales. His voice echoed through the chamber while listening prisoners, jailors, and Genoese guests sat breathless and wide-eyed.

Rustichello followed along, scribbling with pen and ink, filling page after page. He wrote in French, the language most often spoken at royal courts and in polite circles in Europe. "Great Princes, Emperors and Kings," he invited in his prologue, "Dukes and Marquises, Counts, Knights, and Burgesses! People of all degrees who desire to get knowledge of the various . . . regions of the World, take this Book and cause it to be read to you. For ye shall find therein all kinds of wonderful things . . . according to the description of . . . Marco Polo, a wise and noble citizen of Venice, as he saw them with his own eyes." Rustichello titled the book a *Description of the World*. He organized the chapters and sometimes changed words to suit his romantic writing style. But the remarkable contents of the book came from Marco Polo's mind.

Through the winter months the two men worked. Marco Polo's memories revealed an astonishing world thousands of miles to the east that was completely unknown to Europeans. He claimed his travels had taken him all the way to China and the court of Mongol emperor Kublai Khan. In the service of that ruler, Marco Polo had spent years traveling through Asia before finally sailing for home. Using his notes, he described fascinating facts of Asian history and unusual points of geography. The listeners in the prison room whispered in disbelief as he told of such marvels as unicorns, striped lions, and cannibals. He had lived in golden palaces, and he had seen a city so large it had twelve thousand bridges. He had watched black stones burn on fire, and he had tasted nuts as large as a man's head. Strange animals and plants, fantastic riches, and amazing inventions filled every page of Rustichello's growing manuscript.

Chinese engraving of Mongol emperor Kublai Khan

The unicorn and other beasts, from the Travels of Marco Polo

By spring of 1299, the two men finished their writing. Soon afterwards Marco Polo received happy news. The governments of Genoa and Venice had signed a peace treaty. In May the jailors opened the prison doors and freed the Venetian prisoners. With a copy of his book under his arm, Marco Polo returned to Venice. There he resumed his successful career as a merchant. No one knows what became of the Pisan prisoner Rustichello. But the book the two men wrote soon became a medieval best-seller.

People copied the manuscript and translated it into many different languages. Readers marveled at Marco Polo's stories and found them hugely entertaining. They never fully believed his claims, however. They regarded him instead as a teller of tall tales. European scholars dismissed the contents of the book as being impossible. Rustichello had written, "never hath there been . . . any man of any nation, who in his own person hath had so much knowledge and experience of the . . . World and its Wonders as hath this . . . Marco!" But only a handful of wise men were willing to accept the truth of that bold statement.

It would be many years before Europeans fully realized the importance of Marco Polo and his book. Indeed, in his day, the Venetian merchant had seen more of the world than any other human being. Marco

Portrait of Marco Polo

Polo was the first European to cross the continent of Asia and leave a record of what he saw and heard. His adventures carried him into China, Tibet, Burma, Vietnam, Sri Lanka, and India. He visited some regions no other European would see for another six hundred years.

As a result of his fateful meeting with the writer Rustichello, Marco Polo left thinkers and dreamers a great wealth of information. In time, mapmakers used Polo's book to help them chart the world. Aboard the *Santa María* in 1492, Christopher Columbus carefully thumbed through a copy and found hope and guidance within its pages. It seems impossible that one man full of enterprise and courage could have seen and done so much. Even today readers still marvel at the book best known as *The Travels of Marco Polo*.

Before the Polos' expeditions, no European had ever traveled overland across the continent of Asia.

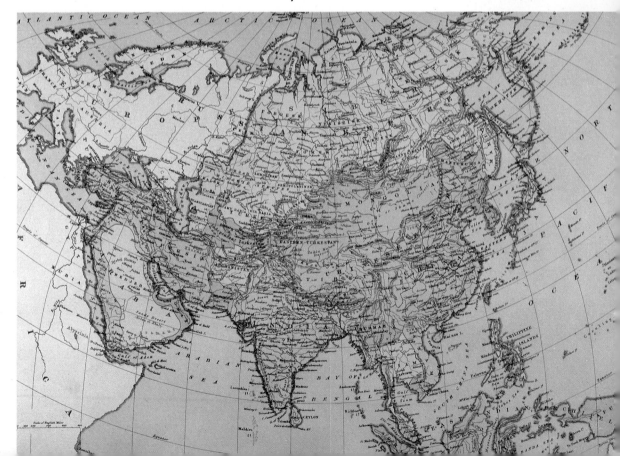

Chapter 2
The Tablet of Gold

S ometime in the year 1254 Marco Polo was born. Smiling servants scurried along the hallways whispering the joyful news, while in a comfortable bedchamber the baby Marco lay cradled in his mother's arms. The Polo house stood in the San Giovanni Chrisostimo district of Venice. By good fortune, Marco had been born into an upper-class family in one of Europe's most exciting cities.

Over the course of seven hundred years, the independent republic of Venice grew on a cluster of marshy islands close by the northeastern coast of present-day Italy. By the middle of the 1200s, the city flourished as an international trading center. Graceful church towers rose into the sky, red-tiled roofs filled the landscape, and the golden doors of splendid palaces glistened in the sunshine. A network of bridges held the islands of the city together. Instead of streets, watery canals often separated plazas and courtyards. Boatmen sang cheerful songs as they steered their narrow gondolas from place to place.

The Polos' home in Venice

At the Rialto, the city's business district, shrewd Venetian merchants haggled over prices. They ran their hands over beautiful bolts of silk, weighed sacks of ground pepper and other spices, and gazed at chained slaves offered for sale. Shiploads of such valuable goods arrived every day from Africa, Arabia, and Asia Minor. In turn, ships sailed from Venice's crowded harbor into the Mediterranean Sea with cargoes bound for every kingdom and country in Europe.

Marco's father, Nicolo, belonged to an ambitious trading family. Nicolo and his brother Maffeo sometimes sailed away from home to trade in foreign ports. Before Marco was born, the two brothers boarded a ship and left Venice again. With chests of valuable merchandise stowed in their vessel's hold, the Polos sailed eastward over the rolling sea. Around the southern tip of Greece the ship glided forward. After several weeks it entered the narrow strait that led to Constantinople (present-day Istanbul, Turkey).

For over one hundred fifty years, religious wars had rocked this portion of the world. Several times, European Christians had organized armies called Crusades to try to free the Holy Land from their Muslim enemies. The people of Venice had supported the Fourth Crusade in 1204 with money. In exchange, they had demanded that the Crusaders attack the rival trading port of Constantinople. The Christian soldiers had plundered the city, looting treasure and burning buildings to the ground.

As Nicolo and Maffeo Polo stepped ashore in 1254, they saw here and there ruined buildings and piles of rubble. But Constantinople still thrived in spite of the destruction it had suffered. The city served as a major trade link between the East and West. Hundreds of

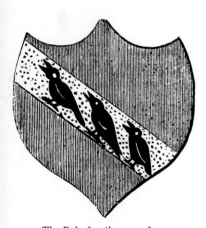

The Polo family coat of arms

16

ships from both the Mediterranean and the Black Sea fought for space in the crowded harbor. Asian caravan routes led overland into the city. Mules and camels packed with ebony, ivory, and colorful silks filed through the narrow streets. The babble of a dozen different languages echoed through the bazaars.

Nicolo and Maffeo Polo joined the large community of Venetians settled in Constantinople. During the next six years the two merchants lived there, skillfully carrying on their business. By 1260, however, violence again threatened Constantinople. Leading Venetians, Genoese, and Greeks all talked of forcefully gaining control of the city. Many worried traders closed their shops. Nicolo and Maffeo also decided it was time to move on. They collected old debts and exchanged their money and goods for jewels.

Venetian Crusaders arriving at Constantinople

The Polo brothers left the troubled city and sailed eastward into the Black Sea. Sea breezes snapped in the sails of their ship as it steered to the port of Soldaia on the Crimean Peninsula. Many overland trade routes led into Soldaia. They stretched across the grassy prairies, or *steppes*, of Russia. The Polo family owned a house in Soldaia, and Nicolo and Maffeo expected to continue their trading there.

Before too long, however, the two brothers realized their mistake. The bazaars of Soldaia proved poorly stocked and offered few opportunities for expert traders. Carefully Nicolo and Maffeo considered their situation. At the time, all routes back to Venice were closed. Pirate ships were lurking in Black Sea coves, too, ready to pounce upon defenseless merchant ships. Reports of wandering bands of thieves kept traders off the roads leading westward. Thus, the Polos decided to travel eastward even farther from Venice. Leading their pack animals ahead, they bravely joined a caravan traveling into the Mongol Empire.

On the high plateau of central Asia, the Mongol people had lived for generations. In hardy bands they thrived as nomads, moving from place to place. Packing up their few belongings, they herded their goats to greener grasslands. Riding like the wind on lean ponies, they expertly tracked wild game, which they shot down with bows and arrows. In the year 1206, the Mongols held a great gathering and elected a new ruler or *khan* to lead their people. They chose a daring chieftain named Genghis. This Genghis Khan soon raised a fearsome army of horsemen. Striking terror in the hearts of their enemies, the Mongol hordes attacked neighboring towns and cities. By 1215, Genghis Khan had taken the capital of Cathay, China's

Genghis Khan

northern province. "The greatest joy a man can know," declared the ruthless khan, "is to conquer his enemies and drive them before him."

Following his victory in Cathay, Genghis Khan set out to conquer the rest of the world. Mongol generals led their armies in all directions. Behind them they left an awful path of death and destruction. They swept south into the Burma Peninsula. In the southwest they conquered much of Persia. In the northwest they galloped across the Russian steppes. Terrified Europeans called the advancing Mongols devils or *Tartars* after Tartarus, the hell of Greek mythology. By 1242, the Tartars had reached the banks of the Danube River in Hungary and had captured the city of Cracow in Poland. For a time Europeans cowered with fear, expecting the worst. But the Tartars finally withdrew in order to strengthen their grip on the territories they had already conquered.

Genghis Khan died in 1227. His sons, grandsons, and loyal generals carried on his conquests and ruled his many kingdoms after him. The trail that Nicolo and Maffeo Polo followed led them to the Volga River in southern Russia. Barka Khan, a grandson of Genghis Khan, ruled this region of the Mongol Empire.

At last the caravan of merchants entered the town of Bolgara. Respectfully Nicolo and Maffeo carried their trade goods into the great tent of Barka Khan. "This Barka was delighted at the arrival of the Two Brothers," explained Marco Polo in his book, "and treated them with great honor; so they presented to him the whole of the jewels that they had brought with them. The Prince was highly pleased with these." Barka Khan rewarded the Polos with gifts that equaled twice the value of the jewels.

The type of war chariot used by the Chinese to battle Genghis Khan

With Barka Khan's permission, the Polo brothers remained in the Volga River region through the next twelve months. The two merchants earned high profits trading in wood, salt, furs, grain, and jewels. Slavery was a common practice in those medieval times. At local slave auctions the Polos probably also bought and sold men and women captured in Mongol battles.

By the spring of 1262, the two Venetians again prepared to return home. Just then, however, war broke out between Barka Khan and his cousin Hulagu Khan, lord of the kingdom to the south. The Polos dared not travel back to Soldaia while lawless bands of Mongols roamed the roads. Instead they pushed eastward, hoping to find a roundabout way home.

The Polos spoke the Mongol language perfectly by this time and felt comfortable with the Mongol culture. Loading their goods onto large, two-wheeled carts called *arabas*, the brothers journeyed deeper into central Asia. After seventeen days of dusty desert roads and blazing heat, they reached the gates of Bukhara. "The city is the best in all Persia," Marco Polo later insisted. "And when they had got thither, they found they could neither proceed further forward nor yet turn back again." Bukhara stood on the frontier of Hulagu Khan's territory, and warfare was a constant threat.

Unable to travel in safety, Nicolo and Maffeo remained for three full years trapped inside Bukhara. Among the shops of the busy marketplace they traded in woven silks, carved ivory, and handsome jewelry while they waited for the danger to end. Finally, ambassadors from the court of Hulagu Khan entered Bukhara. These high officials were traveling to faraway Cathay on a diplomatic mission to Kublai Khan. Since taking the throne in 1260, Kublai Khan, another grandson of Genghis Khan, was respected as the greatest ruler in all of the vast Mongol Empire. While in Bukhara, the ambassadors were surprised to meet the Polos. European Christians (also called Latins, after the official language of the Roman Catholic church) were uncommon in that part of the world.

The ambassadors soon offered the Polo brothers some advice. "The Great Khan hath never seen any Latins, and he hath a great desire so to do," they stated. "Wherefore, if ye will keep us company to his Court, ye may depend upon it that he will be right glad to see you, and will treat you with great honor." In truth, at least two brave Catholic missionaries already had ventured deeply into Asia. Friar Giovanni da Pian del Carpini left Europe in 1245 and Friar Guillaume de Roubrouck began the same difficult journey in 1253. Both men reached the heart of Mongolia and offered to baptize the Mongol people into the Christian faith. Although curious, the Mongol rulers finally sent Carpini and Roubrouck back to Europe. Contact with these European friars, however, made the Asians more curious about the world to the west. In the following years the Mongols more often welcomed adventurous Persians, Turks, and other western traders to their lands.

The first Europeans to take advantage of this new era of open trade, Nicolo and Maffeo grabbed at the chance to leave Bukhara at last. No soldiers or bandits would dare harm merchants traveling in the company of such important ambassadors. With luck, a visit to the fabulous court of the great Kublai Khan would gain them much profit. Once again the brothers packed their trade goods. The walls of Bukhara dropped from their view as they rode eastward.

A long, difficult journey of thousands of miles lay ahead. The caravan stopped at many cities and towns along the winding route. Stubbornly the travelers passed through great stretches of wild, open country, over hills and valleys, and across roaring river fords. Plodding step after step, they crossed snow-covered mountain ranges and the scorching Gobi Desert. Hunger, thirst, danger, and fear remained almost constant companions.

For a full year the Venetian merchants traveled through many strange lands until at last they reached China's Great Wall. The people of Cathay long ago had built this high wall to keep their enemies out. It failed to stop the invading Mongols, though. Now the Polo brothers finished the last part of their journey and became the first Europeans ever known to enter China.

The Polo brothers entering the gates of Bukhara, where they remained for three years

News of the travelers raced ahead from village to town. At last, in 1265, they arrived at the splendid court of Kublai Khan. "When the Two Brothers got to the Great Khan," Marco Polo later revealed in his book, "he received them with great honor and hospitality, and showed much pleasure at their visit." The two merchants enjoyed feasts and entertainments at the Great Khan's court. Gladly they answered all of the questions Kublai Khan curiously asked. He asked them about the emperors of Europe, how they governed, and how they fought their wars. "And then," explained Marco Polo, "he inquired about the Pope and the Church and about all that is done at Rome, and all the customs of the Latins. And the Two Brothers told him the truth in all its particulars, with order and good sense."

The Polos before Kublai Khan

The Christian faith of the Polos interested Kublai Khan. Finally, after months of questions, the Mongol emperor decided to use the Polos as ambassadors to the pope. He drew up letters asking that the pope send to him as many as one hundred Roman Catholic scholars. If these learned men could persuade him that the Christian faith was the best and only true religion, he promised that he and all his people would become Christians. He also asked that the ambassadors bring back sacred oil from the lamp that burned at the traditional burial place of Jesus Christ in the city of Jerusalem in the Holy Land.

The Polo brothers agreed to undertake this difficult mission. It gave them an opportunity to return home at last. Being good Christians, they were honored by the chance to convert the Mongols to their faith. As smart businessmen, they recognized that they might win a special position as traders to the Mongol Empire. To guarantee their safe journey home, Kublai Khan presented his new ambassadors with a tablet of gold. This flattened square of gold was stamped with Kublai Khan's great seal. Words engraved upon the tablet commanded that the ambassadors be given horses, escorts, supplies, and protection all along their route.

In the spring of 1266, Nicolo and Maffeo set forth from Cathay in the company of a Mongol baron named Cogatal. After twenty days of travel, Cogatal fell ill. The Polos journeyed onward without him, protected by their tablet of gold. The westward trip across Asia took the Polo brothers three long years. They survived rainstorms and blizzards. Floods and snows often blocked their route and made progress slow. At last the brave travelers passed out of the Mongol Empire.

Pope Clement IV

After crossing the mountains of Armenia, they reached the Mediterranean port of Ayas in April 1269.

Bad news greeted the Polos as they talked with Italian merchants on the docks. Pope Clement IV had died just a few months earlier. The weary ambassadors possessed important letters from Kublai Khan, but now they could not deliver them. Salt breezes blew into Ayas harbor as they wondered what to do. With longing they gazed across the Mediterranean waves and thought of Venice and home.

The Great Khan giving the Polo brothers a golden tablet as a passport through his kingdom

Chapter 3
Teobaldo of Piacenza

Laughing and shouting with his friends, fifteen-year-old Marco Polo wandered through the streets of Venice. Throughout his childhood he had enjoyed a carefree life. Although his mother had died when he was a baby, his Aunt Flora took him in. He was raised in a house often crowded with cousins and other relatives. During his youth, the only world Marco ever knew was the world of Venice. But what a world that was.

Few Venetian boys stayed in school for very long in those days. Marco probably only studied long enough to learn to read and write. Then he spent his days exploring his island city. "Venice [is] today the most beautiful and the pleasantest city in all the world," exclaimed Martino da Canale, who lived there when Marco Polo was growing up. "Venice is enthroned upon the sea, and . . . from every place come . . . merchants who sell and buy, and money changers and citizens of every craft, and seafaring men of every sort, and vessels to carry [goods] to every port."

At the shipbuilding yards, Marco watched workmen expertly hammer together war galleys and merchant ships. On the harbor wharves he stared at the bags of cinnamon and pepper heaped high. He scrambled among barrels of salt and salted fish and bales of silks and cotton fabric. Looking in at craft shops, Marco saw glassblowers spinning their blowpipes and turning liquid bubbles of glass into bottles. He watched jewelers bend gold and silver into rings and necklaces and observed weavers turning wool, cotton, and silk thread into cloth for dyeing and sewing.

Running through the narrow, muddy streets, Marco brushed past noblemen carried in chairs by servants. To keep mud off their clothes, Venetian ladies wore such tall wooden clogs on their feet that they looked like they were walking on stilts. Often Marco roamed through central St. Mark's Square. On three sides stood busy shops and markets. On the fourth rose the dome of St. Mark's Church. During religious festivals, Marco joined in the celebrations and marched in colorful pageants. Inside the church the boy stared at the vivid mosaics and carved marble. At such solemn moments, he marveled at the glory and the mysteries of his Roman Catholic faith.

More than anything else, the sea that surrounded Venice excited Marco's imagination. At the Rialto he overheard merchants talk of faraway ports. On the docks he dreamily watched boats with high-rigged canvas sails plow through the water as seagulls whirled overhead. Outside taverns he crouched and listened as bearded sailors told stories of sea battles, pirates, and shipwrecks.

Whenever he thought of his long-lost father and uncle, Marco guessed that they were dead. Imagine the teenaged boy's surprise, then, on a certain day in 1269. Perhaps a servant answered the knocking at the door of the Polo family home. Inside stepped a pair of smiling travelers: Nicolo and Maffeo Polo. Relatives blinked their eyes and shouted with joy. The return of the two brothers after fifteen years seemed like a miracle.

It greatly saddened Nicolo Polo to learn that his wife had died. He beamed with pleasure, though, to discover he had a sturdy fifteen-year-old son. The intelligent boy never tired of listening when his father and uncle told of the strange lands they had visited. He asked dozens of questions about the people and customs of those foreign places. When Nicolo and Maffeo talked together in the foreign languages they knew, Marco eagerly began to pick up words and phrases. Excitedly he learned about the Asian caravan routes and the habits of the Mongols. As time passed, Marco came to know all the details of the older Polos' journey. He even understood the importance of their mission for the Mongol ruler Kublai Khan.

The death of Pope Clement IV had upset the plans of Nicolo and Maffeo. After learning the unhappy news at Ayas, they had boarded a ship and sailed to the nearby seaport of Acre. Christian Crusaders held that stretch of the Mediterranean coast. At Acre, the Polo brothers had sought the advice of an important churchman named Teobaldo of Piacenza. As the church's legate, or official representative, in the Holy Land, Teobaldo listened to the travelers' story with great interest. He suggested that Nicolo and Maffeo wait for the election of a new pope. Then he urged that they carry out their mission to Kublai Khan. Such an opportunity to spread the Christian faith should not be lost.

The Polo brothers had agreed to try to follow the wise advice. "But while the Pope is a-making," they had told each other, "we may as well go to Venice and visit our households." Therefore they had journeyed across the sea to their home.

For the next two years the Polo brothers waited for the choosing of the new pope. During that time Nicolo enjoyed the company of his son. He also married a second wife. Neither Nicolo nor Maffeo could settle down completely, however. Thoughts of the wandering life in Asia returned often to their minds. The streets and canals of Venice seemed dull when compared to the wide world they had seen. They knew the Great Khan waited for them in Cathay. Adventure, honors, and riches could be gained, if only they could fulfill their mission.

Finally, in the summer of 1271, the two elder Polos impatiently began packing. They decided to travel to Jerusalem in the Holy Land and obtain the oil requested by Kublai Khan. They hoped that, by the time they completed that task, a new pope would be elected.

One day Nicolo called his son to his side with happy news. He and Maffeo had decided to bring Marco along on their expedition. Having reached the age of seventeen, Marco was now a bright and able young man. It was time he fully learned the merchant's trade in the service of the two older men.

This news thrilled Marco, who had feared he would be left behind. Marco knew this journey would take him from Venice for many years. Still, he eagerly helped his father and uncle with the packing. At last he had his chance to travel. He would visit strange lands and see for himself the fantastic wonders the

older Polos described. Perhaps he would even meet the Great Khan!

At last the day for sailing arrived. Excitedly Marco joined his father and uncle on deck. A breeze flapped in the sails of the vessel as Marco gazed around the harbor. He could not possibly guess what adventures lay ahead of him, but his heart pounded with enthusiasm. During the next days the ship sailed south into the Mediterranean Sea. The sailors aboard spoke nervously of raiding pirates and rough storms. But the ship reached Acre on schedule without encountering any dangers.

The Polos saying good-bye to their friends as they leave Venice, from the Travels of Marco Polo

31

Acre, an important port on the Mediterranean, went back and forth among many conquerors throughout the Middle Ages. Crusaders seized it from the Turks in 1099, but the sultan Saladin took it in 1187. After Richard the Lion-Hearted conquered Acre again in 1191 (above), it became the rich and powerful city that the Polos visited.

Acre probably looked much the same to Marco Polo in 1271 as it did to German traveler Ludolph Von Suchem in about the year 1350. "This glorious city of Acre," described Von Suchem, "stands . . . on the seashore, built of square hewn stones . . . with lofty and exceedingly strong towers." Christian pilgrims stopped at the fortress city of Acre on their way to visit the holy sites of Jerusalem. Now the Polos walked the crowded streets beneath the shade of colorful silk awnings.

At Acre the Polos again visited the churchman Teobaldo of Piacenza. Teobaldo understood the Polos' impatience to return to Kublai Khan. He granted them permission to journey to Jerusalem to fetch some holy oil at the burial site of Jesus Christ. The three Venetians joined the steady stream of travelers heading toward Jerusalem. A sacred city for Jews, Muslims,

Jerusalem's Church of the Holy Sepulcher, built around the spot believed to be Jesus' burial place

and Christians alike, Jerusalem drew devout pilgrims from Europe, the Middle East, and Africa to its religious shrines.

At the cave that was the gravesite of Jesus, the Polos crept inside and obtained some blessed oil from the lamp that burned there. With this gift for Kublai Khan secured, the Polos immediately traveled back to Acre. Marco followed his father and uncle into the church, where they met again with Teobaldo. The older Polos soon explained, "As we see no sign of a Pope's being made, we desire to return to the Great Khan; for we have already tarried long, and there has been more than enough delay." Teobaldo agreed with their decision. He penned letters to the Great Khan stating that the Polos had done their best to carry out his requests.

With letters and oil the Polos set forth, sailing first to the seaport of Ayas. There an excited messenger caught up with them. The cardinals in Rome finally had elected a new pope. The man they had picked was none other than Teobaldo of Piacenza. Taking the new name of Pope Gregory X, Teobaldo directed the Polos to return to Acre for instructions. When the king of Armenia, who controlled Ayas, heard this news, he recognized the Polos as respected ambassadors of the pope. He immediately placed at their command an armed galley ship, which swiftly carried them to Acre.

Teobaldo welcomed the three Venetians with honors and blessings and officially approved their mis-

The Polos before Pope Gregory X

sion. Now, as pope, he drew up new letters of friendship to be delivered to Kublai Khan. Servants wrapped glasses and vases of finely cut crystal to be presented as gifts to the Mongol ruler. The pope wished to send the one hundred Christian scholars requested by the Great Khan, but such a large number was not immediately available. Instead, he assigned two Holy Land friars to accompany the Polos: Brother Nicholas of Vincenza and Brother William of Tripoli. "These were unquestionably as learned Churchmen as were to be found in the Province at that day," wrote Marco afterwards. Pope Gregory X granted the two friars full power to represent the Roman Catholic church in Cathay.

Without further delay, the Polos and the two friars sailed to Ayas. From there they started together on the road toward Armenia's frontier. Unfortunately, word soon reached them that an invading army of Egyptian Muslims was destroying the countryside ahead. The two friars shuddered with fear and refused to travel any farther. A group of Crusaders called the Knights Templars were encamped nearby. Brother Nicholas and Brother William begged for their protection. The good knights agreed to escort the two terrified friars back to the coast.

At the same time, the Polos made their final decision. Nicolo and Maffeo knew the road ahead and spoke the local languages. They possessed impressive letters from the pope and the protective tablet of gold from the Great Khan. The loss of the two friars disappointed them, but they recalled their duty to the khan and filled their hearts with courage. "So," penned the writer Rustichello, "Nicolo and Maffeo and Marco along with them, set out on their journey and rode on."

Chapter 4
The Journey East

"The country contains numerous towns and villages, and has everything in plenty," described Marco Polo. The three Venetian travelers continued ahead, first passing through the region called Lesser Armenia. In order to avoid the rampaging army of Egyptian Muslims, the Polos chose a route that took them northward. This detour led them through the rocky hills of a country called Turcomania (present-day eastern Turkey). They traveled through pasturelands where cattle and horses grazed. In the towns and villages, Marco noticed that the people occupied themselves with trade and handicrafts. "They weave the finest and handsomest carpets in the world, and also a great quantity of fine rich silks."

Seated on horseback and leading their pack mules, the Polos left Turcomania and next entered Greater Armenia, southeast of the Black Sea. In this region jutted the snowcapped peak of Mount Ararat. According to the Bible, Noah's Ark had settled on Mount Ararat after the Great Flood.

Farther to the east, between the Black Sea and the Caspian Sea, lay the region called Georgia. "Towards Georgia," marveled Marco, "there is a fountain from which oil springs in great abundance. . . . This oil is not good to use with food, but 'tis good to burn." People traveled from miles around to collect lamp oil at this early oilfield.

Beyond the reach of warring Muslims, the Polos now turned in a more southerly direction. Their route carried them near the Kingdom of Mosul (part of present-day Iraq). "All the cloths of gold and silk that are called *Mosulins* are made in this country," Marco later explained. Today, closely woven white cotton cloth is still called muslin after this famous weaving region.

South of Mosul stood the city of Baghdad. It is unlikely the Polos traveled through Baghdad. In his book, however, Marco described many places based upon stories he heard along the trail. Baghdad, learned Marco, "is the noblest and greatest city in all those regions." As a center of the Muslim faith, Baghdad had been ruled by men called caliphs for five hundred years. According to the tale Marco later told, Mongols commanded by Hulagu Khan conquered the region in 1255 (actually 1258). Hulagu Khan discovered that the conquered caliph possessed a great pile of treasure. The caliph had hoarded this gold instead of spending it on soldiers to defend his kingdom. As a cruel lesson on greed, Hulagu Khan locked the caliph in a tower with nothing but his treasure. Unable to eat his gold, the caliph soon starved to death.

Along the highway that led south from Georgia, the Polos probably stopped at the city of Tabriz. Lustrous pearls could be bought at the famed Tabriz marketplace. Perhaps Marco learned useful phrases of Arabic and Persian as he bartered with the local merchants. Pressing onward, the Polos may have joined a large trading caravan as they journeyed the dusty roads of Persia (modern-day Iran). Although a caravan offered travelers greater safety, such a long line of loaded camels, packed mules, and horsemen moved only about ten miles (sixteen kilometers) a day.

Hulagu Khan locking up the caliph of Baghdad in his treasure tower

Gradually the Polos wound their way southward. The ruins of Mongol conquest marked many of the cities of Persia. At the city of Saba, the three Venetians stopped and rested. It was said that the Three Wise Men set out from Saba when they went to bring gifts to the baby Jesus at Bethlehem. Marco reported that the three kings lay buried in Saba side by side. Heading farther south, the Polos arrived at the city of Kerman. In the markets of Kerman, Marco saw beautiful turquoise stones that miners chipped from the rocks of the neighboring mountains. The craftsmen of Kerman fashioned handsome spurs and swords from fine steel. On embroidered pillows, quilts, and cushions, Marco declared that "the ladies of the country . . . produce exquisite needlework . . . with figures of beasts and birds, trees and flowers, and a variety of other patterns."

Zebu

From Kerman, the Polos rode south for seven days. The trail led their caravan through a high mountain pass at 10,000 feet (3,048 meters). The temperature plunged at this high altitude and caused the travelers to shiver with cold. Another two days brought them down into the vast, hot Rudbar Plain. In this region, the caravan passed villages, pastures, and groves of swaying date trees. Marco marveled at the strange oxen that he saw. "These are very large, and all over white as snow. . . . The horns are short and thick . . . and between the shoulders they have a round hump. . . . There are no handsomer creatures in the world." Besides this species of humped oxen called the zebu, Marco noticed a kind of large sheep whose tails alone sometimes weighed as much as thirty pounds (fourteen kilograms).

Caravans that traveled across Asia could expect to be attacked by bandits.

Farther south, the road the Polos traveled toward almost certain danger. At night around the campfire, the Polos listened nervously as knowing members of their caravan told of bandits called the *Karaunas*. The sons of Indian mothers and Mongol fathers, the Karaunas terrorized the countryside. In that region, great clouds of blinding dust sometimes choked the air. Local people believed the Karaunas raised these clouds by black magic. Under cover of these storms, the Karaunas often made their attacks. "They know the country thoroughly," Marco later declared, "and ride abreast, keeping near one another, sometimes to the number of 10,000. . . . In this way they extend across the whole plain . . . and catch every living thing that is found outside of the towns and villages; man, woman, or beast, nothing can escape them!"

In spite of the danger, the large caravan continued across the plain. Suddenly one day, in the midst of a dust cloud, the feared army of robbers struck. Taken by surprise, the caravan scattered in all directions. As men yelled all around them, the Polos spurred their horses and galloped toward the nearest village. Wild robbers chased close behind. Just ahead of their attackers, the Polos found protection within the village walls. Altogether, only eight members of the caravan escaped. The Karaunas murdered the rest or carried them off to be sold into slavery.

Grateful to be alive, the Polos gathered up their remaining belongings. Eager to put the awful Rudbar Plain behind them, the three Venetians pressed onward. The weather turned warmer as the Polos neared the Persian Gulf. Parrots cackled a welcome from the heights of date trees. Another week of travel brought the Polos to the seacoast city of Hormuz. At Hormuz the Polos planned to find a ship to carry them eastward across the Indian Ocean. The harbor bustled with activity. "Merchants come thither from India," remarked Marco later, "with ships loaded with spicery and precious stones, pearls, cloths of silk and gold, elephants' teeth, and many other wares."

The quality of the boats docked at Hormuz failed to impress the Polos, however. "Their ships are wretched," declared Marco, "for they have no iron fastenings, and are only stitched together with twine. . . . They have one mast, one sail, and one rudder, and have no deck, but only a cover spread over the cargo. . . . Hence 'tis a perilous business to go a voyage in one of those ships, and many of them are lost, for in the Sea of India the storms are often terrible." For the Polos, the risk of sailing in such a frail vessel seemed too great.

Fishing nets strung out over the Indian Ocean. Fierce storms here can destroy poorly made boats.

Unwilling to travel by sea, the Polos finally decided upon an overland route to Cathay. Bravely the three travelers started back to Kerman. Luckily they avoided meeting the terrible Karaunas as they recrossed the Rudbar Plain. At the crossroads of Kerman, the Polos picked up the trail leading northeast toward the Pamir Mountains. Through the next seven weary days, the travelers plodded across a wide salt desert. Only one gurgling spring provided the men and their animals with refreshment during that time.

The Polos rested at the desert town of Kuhbanan. They refilled their water bags before continuing across another stretch of desert. Eight parched days of heat and dust brought them to the region called Tunokain. After days of stark desert, Marco happily remarked that the natives seemed "a very fine-looking people, especially the women."

The lands beyond Tunokain had been conquered by the Mongols of Hulagu Khan in 1256. During the previous one hundred fifty years, a group of Muslims called the *Assassins* had lived in that region. Marco learned the strange story of the Assassins and told it in his book. A certain Muslim sheik named Alaodin founded the Assassins in 1090. After building a mountain castle, Alaodin laid out a nearby valley with beautiful gardens filled with fruit trees and flowers. Streams of wine, milk, and honey were designed to flow through golden pavilions where lovely maidens danced and sang.

After preparing his enchanting valley, Alaodin—who was also called "The Old Man of the Mountain"—gathered the young men of the countryside. He promised them a glimpse of paradise. The young men were drugged and carried into the valley. When they awoke in the beautiful gardens, they truly believed they had entered paradise. After a few days, Alaodin ordered the young men drugged again. They awakened in his castle but begged for the chance to return to paradise. Slyly Alaodin promised them the reward of eternal paradise if only they would do his bidding. In that manner he obtained the total loyalty of his group called the Assassins.

The Old Man of the Mountain and the leaders who followed in the years after him used the Assassins to spread their power and influence. Following orders, Assassins madly murdered a shah of Persia, a grand vizier of Egypt, two caliphs of Baghdad, leading Crusaders, and other important enemies. Only the capture of the Old Man's castle by Hulagu Khan ended the Assassins's reign of terror. Today, political murderers are still called "assassins."

Arabic/Persian calligraphy in the illustration border:

بیک نگاه تو رستم زنیک نیسی حوش

خوش اگر سوی من افت دنگاه دبست

Hulagu Khan, who slayed the Old Man of the Mountain, sipping on kumiss, his favorite beverage

Northeastward out of Persia, the Polos rode through fruitful valleys and grassy pasturelands. Following the common trade route, they stopped at the city of Shibarghan, in present-day Afghanistan. "It has plenty of everything," Marco afterwards remarked, "but especially of the very best melons in the world." After having their fill of sweet dried melons, the Polos made their way onward to Balkh in northern Afghanistan. Genghis Khan had conquered and destroyed Balkh in 1222. While resting in the ruined ancient city, the Polos walked along the nearly deserted streets and gazed at the blackened marble of crumbling palaces.

The little caravan continued beyond Balkh. After a twelve-day ride, the Polos next rested at a mountain fortress called Taican. The mountains to the south, noted Marco, contained deposits of pure salt. Miners broke it up with iron picks and sold it to people who came from miles away. Farther to the northeast, the travelers entered the province of Badakhshan. Mines in the mountains there yielded shining rubies and sapphires. Marco noted that horse breeders raised excellent horses in that region.

It was Badakhshan's fine climate, however, that most affected the young Venetian. People from the towns and valleys below journeyed to the mountain plateau whenever they fell sick. The crisp air there was so pure that they soon regained their health. The Polos were lucky to reach such a place. While in the foothills of Badakhshan, Marco suffered for nearly a year with illness. Perhaps the hardships of bad food, bad water, and desert travel had struck him down. Fearing for Marco's life, his father and uncle carried him up to the mountain plain. In that restful atmosphere, young Marco soon recovered his health.

The three Polos pressed onward to the northeast. Following the twisting course of the Oxus River, their trail rose higher and higher into the Pamirs. Herds of great wild sheep nibbled at grass among the mountain rocks. The curling horns of the rams were as long as four-and-a-half feet (one-and-a-half meters). Shepherds carved the horns into bowls or piled them up to form pasture fences.

Local natives call the lofty Pamirs the "Roof of the World." Some peaks rise to a height of over 20,000 feet (6,100 meters). High among the mountains, the three Venetians, with their guides and servants, spent twelve days crossing a plateau. The men dressed warmly to fight the biting cold. No birds flew at this high altitude. In camp at night, Marco noticed that "fire does not burn so brightly nor give out so much heat as usual, nor does it cook food so well." It seemed very strange to Marco, but it was actually a natural effect of the thin air at that great height.

At the eastern edge of the plateau, the route sloped downward. During the next weeks the little caravan passed through pleasant valleys and green meadows. The travelers gradually reached the open farmlands and orchards of the Kashgar region. The older Polos nodded their heads with satisfaction. To them this was familiar territory. Beside them Marco breathed the rich, fresh air and gazed with excitement to the east. At last the Polos found themselves on the fringe of China.

Turkestan at the foot of the Pamirs

Chapter 5
"Welcome Is He, Too"

"**K**ashgar is a region lying between north-east and east, and . . . is subject to the Great Khan," explained Marco Polo in his book. The famed caravan trade route called the Silk Route led southeastward out of Kashgar. The Polos followed that road to the ancient city of Khotan.

Beyond Khotan, the Polos watched miners digging in dry riverbeds. The diggers uncovered pieces of yellow, green, and black jade. Carved and polished by Chinese craftsmen, such beautiful stones would bring great prices. As wise businessmen, surely the Polos obtained some fine pieces of jade to carry into China for trading.

The land grew more dry and sparsely settled as the travelers pressed ahead, skirting the southern edge of the Takla Makan Desert. "The whole of the Province is sandy, and so is the road all the way," remarked Marco of the region called Cherchen. In time they rode into the Lop Nor basin at the eastern edge of the Takla Makan. An even greater desert, the Gobi, now lay ahead of them. Nicolo and Maffeo had trekked across the Gobi before and knew its dangers. At Lop Nor, the three Venetians rested their mules and camels and gathered supplies for the long desert journey. After a week of careful preparation, they joined a caravan heading east into the Gobi.

"The length of this Desert [from north to south]," declared Marco, "is so great that 'tis said it would take a year and more to ride from one end of it to the other. And here, where its breadth is least, it takes a month to cross it. 'Tis all composed of hills and valleys of sand, and not a thing to eat is to be found on it." As far as Marco could tell, no birds or wild animals lived in this desert. The caravan plodded over sand dunes along the established trail. At intervals on the route lay some twenty-eight waterholes, where men and beasts gladly stopped to gulp fresh water.

From his fellow travelers Marco heard scary stories of evil desert spirits. If at night a traveler lagged behind a moving caravan and lost sight of it, spirit

Sand dunes and oasis near Dunhuang, China, formerly called Shachow

voices and false caravan noises would lead him astray. "Sometimes the spirits will call him by name," Marco later claimed. "Even in the day-time one hears the sound of a variety of musical instruments." Perhaps as the Polos crossed the hazy desert, the whistling winds and shifting sands played tricks on their tired senses. Visions of "mirages" and the sound of "singing sands" are long traditions of the desert.

Asbestos ore

For thirty days the caravan crossed the drifting dunes. The sun beat down with sweltering cruelty. Gusts of wind raised blinding clouds of sand. All the animals wore bells around their necks so they would not get lost at night. Each morning the travelers hastily broke camp, eager to finish their difficult journey.

The Polos smiled gratefully when the caravan finally reached the eastern edge of the Gobi Desert. Before them rose the walls of the city of Shachow (present-day Dunhuang). As the caravan entered the city gates, Marco gazed upon Chinese people for the first time.

Refreshed by their stay in Shachow, the Polos continued eastward. To the north lay a district called Chinghintalas. A Turkish merchant traveling with the Polos' caravan had lived for a time in that region. He told Marco of a remarkable substance dug from the mountains there. Miners dug the material out, crushed it, and washed it clean. Divided into fibers like wool, the substance then was spun and woven into cloth. The amazing thing was that it would not burn when thrust into fire. Clearly this startling substance was none other than asbestos. In modern times, builders used this fireproof material in construction, until doctors discovered that breathing asbestos fibers is very dangerous to people's health.

Yak

The Polos visited the Chinese city of Kanchow (modern-day Lanzhou) and followed the road leading deeper into Cathay. Strange animals found in this region fascinated Marco. Great shaggy beasts called yaks yielded a fine wool for weaving. From a gland in one variety of little antelope came a fragrant substance called musk, which was sold as a valued perfume.

Here Marco noticed increasing evidence of the Mongols. The Mongol people still lived the nomad life. To escape the winter cold of Mongolia, they herded their cattle southward onto the Chinese plains. In summer they returned to the north to enjoy the cool climate of mountain meadows. As the Polos passed among Mongol camps, Marco learned all he could about their culture.

The Mongols lived in great round tents called yurts. Wooden poles formed the frames, and these were covered with walls and roofs of felt fabric. When the time for moving arrived, the Mongols took apart their yurts and load them onto wagons. "These are drawn by oxen and camels," explained Marco, "and the women and children travel in them." The horsemen rode beside, herding flocks of goats and sheep. "They live on the meat which their herds supply," observed Marco. "Their drink is mare's milk, prepared in such a way that you would take it for white wine; and a right good drink it is, called by them *kumiss.*"

Mongol women worked hard. They cut and dried meat and churned butter. They pounded sheep wool into felt and stitched boots and bags from horsehide leather. Riding horseback, the women often tended the herds. For their part, it seemed the Mongol men lived for hunting and fighting. With shining eyes, they chased wild game across the plains or expertly wheeled their ponies in practice troop formations.

Interior of a yurt, in the Islamic Museum, Istanbul, Turkey

Mongols transporting a yurt on an ox-drawn wagon

"They are stout fighters," Marco later declared. "Their weapons are bows and swords and clubs; but they rely mainly on their bows, for they are excellent archers. On their backs they wear an armor of buffalo hide or some other leather which is very tough."

During times of war, the Mongols showed their true toughness. "If need be," marveled Marco, "they will go for a month without any supply of food, living only on the milk of their mares and on such game as their bows may win them. Their horses also will subsist entirely on the grass of the plains, so that there is no need to carry . . . barley or straw or oats." The skillfully organized Mongols traveled light and fought ruthlessly in battle. After observing these warriors, Marco better understood why "they are masters of the biggest half of the world."

As travelers, the three Polos had proven their own hardiness. For three-and-a-half years they had endured mountains, deserts, plains, hunger, illness, and danger. But at last they were nearing their goal. One day in the spring of 1275, a cloud of dust rose upon the road ahead. Soon a troop of horsemen halted beside them. News of the Polos had reached the Great Khan, and he sent these soldiers to escort them the rest of the way. For the next forty days, the three Venetians traveled in a manner befitting royal ambassadors. At every inn where they stopped, delicious foods and comfortable beds awaited them. Each morning they mounted fresh horses and rode onward.

On the fortieth day, the city of Shangtu appeared on the horizon. Before long, the horsemen and pack animals trotted through the high city gates. Marco held his breath with expectation as they approached the beautiful summer palace of the Great Khan. There the three Venetians climbed marble steps and were led along golden halls. Marco's feelings of thrilled wonder increased with every step, until at last they entered the great court chamber. On a high throne sat Kublai Khan with dozens of barons standing about him in respectful attendance.

The three travelers stepped forward. They humbly dropped to their knees and bowed their heads to the floor. Graciously the Mongol emperor bade them rise. He showed great pleasure at seeing Nicolo and Maffeo again after so many years. He asked them many questions about their journeys and about their meetings with the pope. Nicolo and Maffeo answered as best as they could. They presented to the Great Khan the documents, letters, and gifts sent by Pope Gregory X. They unwrapped and set before him the sacred oil they had brought from Jerusalem. The Great Khan was not at all upset that the Polo brothers had not brought one hundred Christian scholars with them. Instead he warmly thanked the two men for having accomplished so much.

Gazing at the travelers, Kublai Khan noticed Marco standing silent and respectful behind his father and uncle. Curiously he asked who the young man was.

"Sire," answered Nicolo, "he is my son and your servant."

The emperor looked again at the twenty-year-old who stood with a noble posture and dark, intelligent eyes.

"Welcome is he, too," announced the Great Khan with a smile.

At that moment Marco Polo could hardly guess that he would spend the next seventeen years in faithful service to the great Mongol ruler.

Drawing of the Great Khan's palace, from the Travels of Marco Polo

Chapter 6
Life at Court

The Great Khan ordered a fabulous feast that night to celebrate the return of the Polos. Marco sat with his father and uncle in a place of honor, eating delicious foods and watching colorful entertainments. Then and many times afterwards, Marco had a chance to observe the nearly sixty-year-old Kublai Khan. "He is a man of good stature," he described, "neither short nor tall but of moderate height. . . . His complexion is fair and ruddy like a rose, the eyes black and handsome, the nose shapely and set squarely in place."

Less brutal than the Mongol rulers before him, Kublai Khan preferred the luxuries of Chinese civilization to life on the Mongolian plains. Therefore he established his capital city at Khanbalik in Cathay (the present-day city of Beijing in the Peoples Republic of China). During the winter months the Great Khan remained at Khanbalik. Each spring he enjoyed a great hunting expedition into the region near the Yellow Sea. The months of June, July, and August, however, always found the emperor at his summer palace at Shangtu.

Kublai Khan's marble palace at Shangtu greatly impressed Marco Polo. "The rooms," Marco declared, "are all gilt and painted with figures of men and beasts and birds, and with a variety of trees and flowers, all executed with such exquisite art that you regard them with delight and astonishment." This grand marble palace served as the entrance to the Great Khan's private park. The walls surrounding this park extended sixteen miles (twenty-six kilometers). "Inside the Park," Marco soon learned, "there are fountains and rivers and brooks, and beautiful meadows."

Gamekeepers kept the park stocked with deer and other wild animals for hunting. For the emperor's

Kublai Khan, with his cheetah behind him, using a falcon to hunt wild game

pleasure, they also had two hundred falcons and hawks in cages. "The Khan himself goes every week to see his birds," Marco later recalled. When they were let loose, the emperor enjoyed watching them swoop from the sky as they hunted after prey. Marco never forgot the sight of the emperor on horseback. Behind his seat he often kept tied a half-tamed cheetah. When he spied distant wild game, he unleashed the cheetah, which sprang off and killed the animal. This unusual method of hunting greatly amused Kublai Khan.

In the midst of this game park stood a second palace built of bamboo cane. This splendid palace was decorated with golden dragons. The lacquered bamboo roof was completely waterproof, and sturdy ropes of silk braced the walls. Servants could take apart this bamboo palace and move it anywhere in the park the Great Khan commanded. Often after a day of hunting, the emperor chose to stay in his bamboo palace rather than return to the marble palace.

Following his yearly schedule, the Great Khan left Shangtu on August 28. The Polos joined the thousands of members of the emperor's court as they followed him south to the capital. The cavalcade of courtiers stretched miles along the road. Always Marco stared ahead, eager to see Khanbalik, about which he had so often heard. In time they reached the busy suburbs of the fabled capital city. Standing forty-five feet (13.7 meters) high, the thick outer walls of Khanbalik rose in the distance. The four walls of the city each stretched six miles, making a giant square totaling twenty-four miles (39 kilometers) in perimeter. Twelve massive gateways guarded by soldiers stood at regular intervals. At last the Polos rode through one of these and into Khanbalik.

The city of Khanbalik, on the site of present-day Beijing

The grand design of the city thrilled Marco instantly. "The streets are so straight and wide," he later exclaimed, "that you can see right along them from end to end and from one gate to the other. And up and down the city there are beautiful palaces . . . and fine houses in great numbers. . . . The whole city is arranged in squares just like a chessboard." Such perfect order seemed amazing to someone used to the twisting, haphazard streets and canals of Venice. The huge population of Khanbalik surprised Marco as well. People crowded the streets, shops, and marketplaces. Merchants from throughout Cathay brought their goods to trade in Khanbalik. Every day of the year, Marco later declared, at least one thousand cartloads of raw silk were wheeled into the city and sold to clothmakers. In the center of the city stood a great

The Temple of Heaven was built in Beijing after the fall of the Mongol Empire. The temple's squared lines represent earth and the circular lines represent heaven.

bell. Every night, the third time the bell was struck marked the start of curfew. Afterwards, only nurses with lanterns on their way to assist the sick were allowed on the streets. In the darkness, the great city of Khanbalik fell quiet.

Within the city stood the walls of the Great Khan's Imperial Palace. "You must know," declared Marco, "that it is the greatest Palace that ever was." The whitewashed outer walls around this palace covered a total length of four miles (6.4 kilometers). A second set of walls lay within. "Between the two walls of the enclosure," revealed Marco, "are fine parks and beautiful trees bearing a variety of fruit." Deer wandered about these parks, squirrels nibbled on nuts, and officers of the Great Khan's imperial guard exercised their horses there.

Stepping inside the inner walls, Marco beheld the Imperial Palace. The stunning, single-story building stood on a raised terrace. "The outside roof," Marco declared, "is all colored with vermilion and yellow and green and blue and other hues, which are fixed with a varnish so fine and exquisite that they shine like crystal."

Inside the palace, Marco gazed at walls covered with gold and silver. On these walls were painted detailed scenes of dragons, beasts and birds, and knights. "And on the ceiling, too," marveled Marco, "you see nothing but gold and silver and painting."

Behind the Imperial Palace, a bubbling stream flowed into a manmade lake that was stocked with fish. Farther away stood a large hill called Green Mount. By order of the emperor, this hill was covered with beautiful evergreens. "And I assure you," Marco later insisted, "that wherever a beautiful tree may exist, and the Emperor gets news of it, he sends for it and has it transported bodily with all its roots and the earth attached to them, and planted on that hill of his." Within this perfect park of evergreens, the Great Khan had built another fine palace painted green inside and out. Often he rode among the peaceful evergreens and relaxed at this green palace.

Marco learned that Kublai Khan had four wives, whom he treated equally. By these wives he had twenty-two sons. The eldest son, Chinkim, possessed a beautiful palace of his own. Great retinues of attendants followed and obeyed these empresses and princes. Often the Great Khan called wives, sons, noblemen, and courtiers to join him in his banquet hall. This giant dining room could seat more than six thousand people.

"And when the Great Khan sits at table on any great court occasion," exclaimed Marco, "it is in this fashion. His table is elevated a good deal above the others, and he sits at the north end of the hall, looking towards the south." From this high perch, the emperor gazed across the entire room. Beside him at a lower level sat sons, nephews, and other relatives. Before him at even lower tables sat noblemen and ladies. Farther away, soldiers and officers sat on rich carpets on the floor. Giant guards stood at the doors of the banquet hall. Outside, a crowd of as many as forty thousand people waited for a chance to present the Great Khan with gifts and to pay their respect.

Kublai Khan on his throne

Great barons of the court served the emperor his meals. Carefully they muffled their noses and mouths with silk handkerchiefs. This prevented the chance of even a single breath spoiling the Great Khan's drink or food. The emperor kept a herd of more than ten thousand white horses. The milk of the mares was made into the Great Khan's favorite drink, kumiss. He sipped this liquor from a handsome golden goblet. Every time he lifted the cup to his lips, musicians in the hall played their instruments. At that signal, everyone knelt and bowed their heads to the floor with deep respect until the emperor finished drinking.

A drawing of Chinese sorcerers working their magic

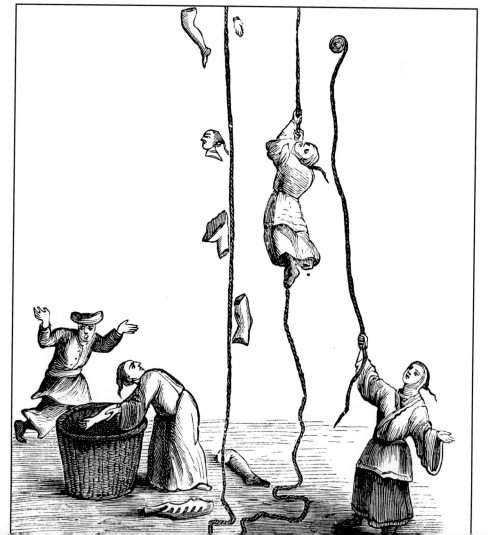

During the meal, magicians from the provinces of Tibet and Kashmir sometimes entertained the crowd. Marco watched with amazement when these sorcerers sent drinking cups floating through the air. At the end of evening banquets, laughter echoed through the hall as actors, jugglers, and acrobats performed.

Marco witnessed many celebrations during his time in Cathay. "The Great Khan was born on the 28th day of . . . September," revealed Marco, "so on that day is held the greatest feast of the year at the Khan's court." On his birthday Kublai Khan dressed in a splendid robe covered with dazzling figures of beaten gold. Twelve thousand of his highest ranking barons also dressed in gold-colored uniforms with golden belts and often ornamented with costly gemstones and shining pearls. From throughout the Mongol Empire, ambassadors and noblemen arrived at Khanbalik. Many presented the Great Khan with chests of gold and other valuables as their yearly taxes. Others gave gifts of treasure in the hope of receiving favor from the emperor.

Another great festival in Cathay occurred on New Year's Day. On that day the Great Khan and his noblemen dressed in white. In fact, explained Marco, "everybody is in white, men and women, great and small . . . for they deem that white clothing is lucky." On New Year's Day a fabulous parade of the emperor's five thousand elephants passed through the streets of Khanbalik. From throughout the empire, the Great Khan received good-luck gifts, including thousands of white horses. "And," declared Marco, "the people also make presents to each other of white things, and embrace and kiss and make merry, and wish each other happiness and good luck for the coming year."

The Great Khan happily spent the first months of every year hunting in the region around Khanbalik. The emperor possessed many trained cheetahs to chase after wild game. "He hath also," described Marco, "several great Lions, bigger than those of Babylonia, beasts whose skins are colored in the most beautiful way, being striped all along the sides with black, red, and white." Surely these striped lions were actually tigers, never seen before in Europe. The spectacle of these tigers chasing and attacking wild boars and other animals filled Marco with awe. "'Tis a rare sight, I can tell you," he afterwards exclaimed.

Each year on the first of March, Kublai Khan set off on a grand, three-month hunting expedition toward the Yellow Sea. "The Emperor himself," explained Marco, "is carried upon four elephants in a fine chamber made of timber, lined inside with plates of beaten gold." The Great Khan sometimes suffered from gout, or swollen joints, and this traveling method allowed him to stretch out on a couch and relax.

At his camping ground, the emperor enjoyed the comforts of a tent large enough to shelter a thousand people. Servants pitched other smaller tents on the plain for the many courtiers in the hunting party. The emperor remained encamped until the end of May. "And all that time," declared Marco, "he does nothing but go hawking round about among the canebrakes along the lakes and rivers that abound in that region." Wild game including rabbits, deer, cranes, and swans thrived at this private imperial game preserve. "The whole country swarms with it," marveled Marco, "and the Emperor gets as much as he could desire."

It seemed that the Great Khan spent much time in hunting and hawking. But the emperor also showed

himself to be a kind and thoughtful ruler. Sometimes bad weather, crop diseases, or locusts destroyed farmers' fields. The Great Khan excused the victims of such misfortunes from paying taxes. Instead he ordered that food and seed be distributed to them from the imperial grain storehouses. Unlucky families received supplies of clothing, too. At the doors of the Imperial Palace in Khanbalik servants also handed out freshly baked loaves of bread and bowls of rice to the needy. "Nobody is denied," declared Marco. "And so some 30,000 people go for it every day from year's end to year's end."

Kublai Khan traveling on the backs of four elephants, from the Travels of Marco Polo

Siddhartha Gautama ("the Buddha"), founder of Buddhism, renounced his princely life for a spiritual life.

By Kublai Khan's command, workmen built hospitals and schools. Rows of trees he had planted along the highways provided travelers with cooling shade and easy-to-see landmarks. After years of labor, crews put to work by the Great Khan dredged a grand canal from Khanbalik to the city of Kinsai (now Hangzhou). The thousands of ships that sailed this waterway greatly increased trade throughout the empire. The ancient teachings of Buddha guided the religious lives of most Chinese. But Kublai Khan tolerated all of the religions practiced in his realm. For the mystical astrologers who served at his court, he built a high observatory so they could better study and chart the stars.

Life in Cathay greatly interested Marco. He noticed that children showed their parents deep respect and looked after them in old age. Marco also saw that the Chinese were a very cleanly people. Everyone soaked in a hot bath at least three times a week and every day in the winter. Europeans never bathed so much. Even more amazing to Marco was the fuel the Chinese used to heat the bathhouse water. "All over the country of Cathay," he exclaimed, "there is a kind of black stones existing in veins in the mountains, which they dig out and burn like firewood." The black stones could keep a fire burning all night long and gave more heat than firewood. Many Europeans learned about coal for the first time when they read of these black stones in Marco's book.

Coal mining in northern China

Mulberry tree—its leaves are food for silkworms, and its bark was the source for Chinese paper money.

Another unusual feature of Chinese society was the use of paper money. Workers stripped the inner bark of mulberry trees, soaked and pounded it into pulp, and made it into paper. At the Emperor's Mint in Khanbalik, workers cut the paper into rectangles of different sizes. Each size signified a different value of money. Mint officials signed their names and stamped each note. Finally the chief official marked every note with the red seal of the Great Khan. Throughout all of the kingdoms, provinces, and territories of his empire, the Great Khan ordered that these paper notes be accepted. Old, ripped, or flimsy notes could be exchanged at the mint for fresh new ones for a small charge. Marco seemed to believe the vast pile of gold and silver in the Imperial Treasury belonged to the Great Khan. In truth, the precious metals backed up the value of the people's paper notes.

Every day at Khanbalik, Marco watched runners and horsemen arrive with packages and messages for the Great Khan. The Chinese system of post express carried mail with astonishing speed. A fabulous network of post stations lay spread along the roads throughout the provinces. Runners with less important dispatches ran three-mile (five-kilometer) relays from station to station. "Everyone of those runners," exclaimed Marco with wonder, "wears a great wide belt, set all over with bells." The noise of the jingling bells alerted the next runner to get ready. Mail speeding along from runner to runner in this manner could make a ten-day journey in a single day.

Riders with more important business traveled even faster. Marco exclaimed that three hundred thousand horses stood corralled at ten thousand way-stations spread across the empire. A horseman galloped twenty-five miles (forty kilometers) or more before passing his mail pouch to the next rider on a fresh horse. Some emergency messages demanded even greater haste. In those cases a single daring rider galloped the entire distance himself, quickly switching horses every few miles along the way.

This impressive system of communications kept the Great Khan in contact with every corner of his empire. Runners brought him fresh fruit from far-off places as soon as it was ripe. Messengers on lathered horses delivered news of distant uprisings and warfare so that the emperor could respond swiftly. With close and wise attention, Kublai Khan controlled his empire. It was not long after the arrival of the Polos that the Great Khan found a way to use the talents of Marco Polo. Soon the curious Venetian was traveling along the empire's roads himself.

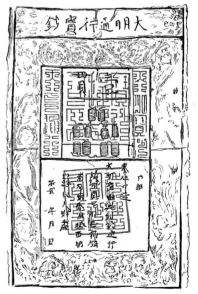

An example of early Chinese paper money

Chapter 7
Marco the Ambassador

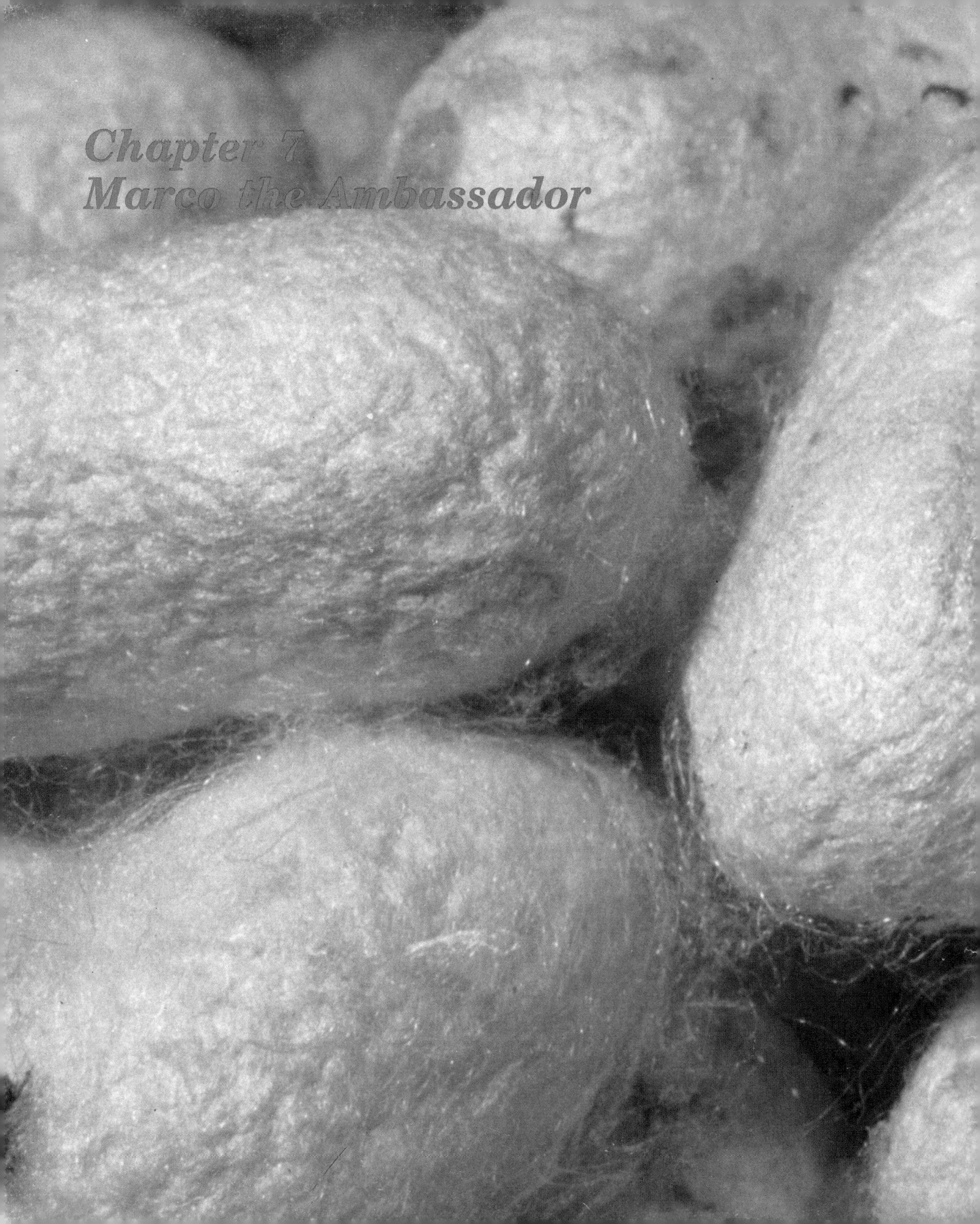

Marco Polo took part in the Great Khan's hunting expeditions. He traveled with the royal court when it moved from Khanbalik to Shangtu. With a keen and curious mind, he quickly learned the Mongol language and the methods of the imperial government. At court, Marco's noble manner and careful conduct soon caught the eye of Kublai Khan.

Often the Great Khan sent ambassadors on business to distant parts of his empire. When they returned from their missions he closely questioned them. "They were able to tell him nothing," Marco soon noticed, "except the business on which they had gone." Openly the Great Khan complained that these men were fools. He wished above all to learn of the strange countries his ambassadors passed through, the unusual sights and peculiar habits of the people. Finally the Great Khan decided to send bright young Marco Polo on a mission. Honored by this trust, Marco silently vowed to learn all he could of the places he visited and to take careful notes.

"Now you must know," penned the writer Rustichello in Marco's book, "that the Emperor sent . . . Marco Polo, who is the author of this whole story, on business of his into the Western Provinces. On that occasion he traveled from Khanbalik a good four months' journey . . . and so now I will tell you all that he saw on his travels as he went and returned." Probably with servants, guides, official documents, and a tablet of gold to prove his importance, Marco rode to the southwest.

Just ten miles (sixteen kilometers) from Khanbalik, Marco reached a wide river called the Hun-Ho. "Over this River there is a very fine stone bridge," Marco later declared, "so fine indeed, that it has very few equals." Twenty-four arches supported the bridge, which was nearly 300 yards (274 meters) long. The bridge's wide roadway provided enough space for ten horsemen to ride along side by side. As he crossed, Marco admired the handsome marble finish and the giant sculpted lions that decorated the bridge.

Upon the road again, Marco journeyed through the fertile valleys of Cathay. His route took him through the cities of Cho-chow, T'ai-yuan-fu, and P'ing-yang-fu. As an ambassador of the Great Khan, everywhere he received courtesy and great respect.

Crossing the Hwang-Ho (Yellow River) after perhaps a month, Marco and his party entered the province of Si-ngan-fu (now Shaanxi province). The silk trade occupied many of the people of this region. Marco noticed "fine plains planted with mulberries, which are the trees on the leaves of which the silkworms do feed." Thriving on their diets of mulberry leaves, the silkworms spun the fine silk threads that were later woven into cloth.

In the provincial museum of Shaanxi (called Si-ngan-fu by Marco Polo) is a collection of stone tablets. One of them, called the Nestorian monument, bears the design of this cross. Dating from the 700s, it was left by Christian missionaries.

Silk-making in China

In the capital city of Si-ngan-fu (present-day Xi'an), weavers turned out lustrous bolts of colored silks, and merchants loaded wagons in order to sell the cloth throughout the empire. The ruler of Si-ngan-fu province was Mangalai Khan, one of Kublai Khan's sons. Marco stayed for a time at his palace. "It stands in a great plain abounding in lakes and streams and springs of water." The palace stood inside a massive wall, its halls and chambers painted and decorated with gold. This palace was "so great and fine that no one could imagine a finer," declared Marco, adding, "This Mangalai rules his realm right well with justice . . . and is much beloved by his people."

Fully rested, Marco continued his journey on a course that led him even farther to the southwest. Mile after mile, he gazed about the countryside with curious interest. Within a few weeks the great plains swelled into hills and then jutted into mountain cliffs. At last the young ambassador stopped at the city of Ch'eng-tu-fu (modern-day Chongqing). This city lay on the banks of the mighty Yangtze River. The vast number of merchant ships on the water greatly surprised Marco. The Yangtze was so big, he exclaimed, "that it seems to be a Sea rather than a River!"

A great half-mile stone bridge crossed the Yangtze here. "The bridge is roofed over from end to end with timber . . . all richly painted." On the bridge stood a customs house, where officials of the emperor collected tolls and taxes from travelers.

Five days' travel beyond the Yangtze River, Marco reached the outer limits of Cathay. Farther to the west rose the craggy mountains of Tibet. Years of war against the Mongols had destroyed much of this region. The poor people here traded with bags of salt instead of money. "They are very poorly clad," remarked Marco, "for their clothes are only of the skins of beasts." Wild animals prowled through the forests of bamboo cane that grew in this country.

Marco soon learned how travelers protected themselves at night. They chopped the bamboo cane and threw it into their fires. The bamboo stalks grew in jointed sections, and the heat of the fire made one section after another suddenly burst open. "They make such loud reports," exclaimed Marco, "that the lions and bears and other wild beasts are greatly frightened, and make off as fast as possible." The noise of the exploding cane crackled so loudly that some trav-

A rare white Asian tiger

elers stuffed their ears with cotton. But at least they could journey through this wild region with safety.

In time, Marco entered the large province of Karajang (modern-day Yunnan), which was ruled by one of Kublai Khan's grandsons, Essen Temur. Karajang marked the goal of Marco's journey. The Great Khan wished to have an eyewitness report on conditions in that conquered Chinese province. Marco noticed many things during his stay in Karajang. In the towns and villages, merchants, craftsmen, and farmers lived well and horse breeders raised excellent horses. The people drank rice wine and liked to eat their meat raw. Instead of gold or the Great Khan's paper notes, the natives of Karajang used small seashells for money.

The province of Karajang covered so much territory it was divided into seven kingdoms. Marco traveled farther southwest into the region where one of the Great Khan's sons, Hukaji Khan, ruled the city of Karajang. Here Marco saw for the first time frightening "snakes and serpents of . . . vast size." "You may be sure," he later exclaimed, "that some of them are ten paces in length. . . . They have two forelegs near the head. . . . The head is very big, and the eyes are bigger than a great loaf of bread. The mouth is large enough to swallow a man whole, and is garnished with great [pointed] teeth. And in short they are so fierce-looking and so hideously ugly, that every man and beast must stand in fear and trembling of them." With sharpened stakes partly buried in the mud, hunters speared these monsters—really crocodiles— as they slithered along the riverbanks.

The people of Karajang could be frightening, too. In years past, before the Great Khan conquered them, they often murdered noble guests with poison. They believed they could capture a man's "good shadow" in this fashion. Thereafter the dead man's fine manners, intelligence, and soul would remain forever to bless the house where he was murdered. The Great Khan, however, outlawed this evil practice.

Once his business was done in Karajang, curiosity drew the young ambassador even farther south into the province of Zardandan. The people of Zardandan surprised Marco with several of their customs. Many of the men wore gold caps over their teeth, "both the upper teeth and the under." They also decorated their arms and legs with bands of black tattoos. "They take five needles joined together," explained Marco, "and with these they prick the flesh till the blood comes, and then they rub in a certain black coloring stuff." The markings lasted forever under the skin, marveled Marco.

Most amazing of all was how Zardandan husbands behaved when their wives had babies. "When one of their wives has been delivered of a child," commented Marco, "the infant is washed and swathed, and then the woman gets up and goes about her household affairs, whilst the husband takes to bed with the child by his side." For an entire forty-day period, the father remained in bed looking after the baby, while friends and family visited to celebrate the birth. "They do this," explained Marco, "because, say they, the woman has had a hard [time] of it, and 'tis but fair the man should have his share of suffering."

Beyond Zardandan lay the Kingdom of Burma. It is possible Marco visited there, too. In the year 1272, the Burmese king had decided to attack the Mongol army advancing through Zardandan. Marco soon learned the story of that battle. "This king prepared a great force," he later described, "and he had, let me tell you, 2,000 great elephants, on each of which was set a tower of timber, well framed and strong, and carrying from twelve to sixteen well-armed fighting men. And besides these, he had of horsemen and of footmen good 60,000 men." This great force marched against an army of just twelve thousand Mongol horsemen.

The Mongol horses snorted and reared backward in fear as the Burmese elephants advanced across an open plain. Wisely the Mongol general Nasr-udden ordered his troops to dismount in a nearby forest and tie the horses to the trees. Then he commanded his soldiers to fire their bows with fury. "They did as he bade them," related Marco, "and plied their bows

Idols on the bank of the Irrawaddy River in Burma

stoutly. . . . And what shall I tell you? Understand that when the elephants felt the smart of those arrows that pelted them like rain, they turned tail and fled . . . with such a noise and uproar that you would have [thought] the world was coming to an end! . . . They plunged into the wood and rushed this way and that, dashing their [towers] against the trees, bursting their harness and smashing and destroying everything that was on them."

The Burmese horsemen and foot soldiers panicked as the Mongols next charged among them on horseback. Mongol warriors sent clouds of arrows whizzing through the air and slashed ahead with their swords until the Burmese retreated in total defeat. Before long, the Mongols had conquered much of Burma.

While in Burma, Marco learned that Burmese noblemen were sometimes entombed in high-storied

Towering pagodas rise over the city of Pegu in Burma.

towers called *pagotas* when they died. The Burmese people wore tattoos of lions, dragons, and birds. The inky markings often decorated every part of their bodies, including their faces. "Those who have the largest amount," declared Marco, "are regarded with the greatest admiration."

Many wild animals lurked in the steaming jungles of Burma. "The country," Marco exclaimed, "swarms with lions to that degree that no man can venture to sleep outside his house at night." To protect themselves from these lions (actually tigers), the Burmese raised a breed of large, fierce dogs. "Every man who goes on a journey takes with him a couple of those dogs, and when a lion appears they have at him with the greatest boldness." Snapping at the animal's legs and rump, the dogs kept the ferocious beast busy until the traveler could kill it with arrows.

Chapter 8
A Second Mission for the Great Khan

Through four months of travel, Marco Polo saw and noted many things in the southwestern region of the Great Khan's empire. The time arrived at last for the young ambassador to return to Khanbalik. In *The Travels* Rustichello revealed, "When Marco returned from his [mission] he presented himself before the Emperor, and after making his report of the business with which he was charged, and its successful accomplishment, he went on to give an account in a pleasant and intelligent manner of all the novelties and strange things that he had seen and heard."

The Great Khan listened to Marco's skillful speech and then announced with amazement: "If this young man live, he can not fail to be a person of great worth and ability." Immediately he granted Marco a noble title and an important place at court.

During the next seventeen long years, Marco remained in the service of the Great Khan. His diplomatic missions carried him to the many kingdoms of the Mongol Empire. Sometimes his father and uncle joined him on his travels. Probably the emperor used the two older Venetians as ambassadors on separate journeys, too. But he trusted Marco the most. On every trip, Marco gathered information useful to the Great Khan. "Then on his return to Court," explained Rustichello, "he would relate everything in regular order, and thus the Emperor came to hold him in great love and favor."

One mission for the Great Khan carried Marco hundreds of miles southeast of Khanbalik into the Chinese province of Manzi. At the head of his servants Marco rode through the countryside. As he passed along, he watched farmers hoe their fields and encountered merchants carrying the trade goods of their region. He examined the quality of the local handicrafts and tasted sweet orchard fruits. He observed religious ceremonies, attended military maneuvers, and visited with princes and noblemen. Everywhere he made his notes, describing the people, their businesses, and the geography of the region.

Before reaching the border of Manzi, Marco traveled through the city of Chang-Lu (present-day Cangzhou). The salty earth found there provided many people with work. "This they dig up," explained Marco, "and pile in great heaps. Upon these heaps they pour water in quantities till it runs out at the bottom; and then they take up this water and boil it well in great iron cauldrons, and as it cools it deposits a fine white salt in very small grains." Merchants sold this salt at great profit in regions where no salt could be found.

A fierce Mongol general named Bayan had conquered Manzi so that the province could be added to Kublai Khan's empire. As Marco traveled along, he soon believed Manzi was the richest province in all of the Eastern World. Leather workers cut and stitched harnesses for horses and armor for soldiers in the city of Yangchow (modern-day Yangzhou). In his book Marco claimed he served as governor of Yangchow for three years by order of the Great Khan. Historians today, however, can find no mention among Chinese records that Marco actually performed the duties of Yangchow governor.

Suzhou, one of the oldest cities in China, is noted for its bridges, gardens, temples, and pagodas. Here is shown the Lingering Garden.

Traveling farther to the southeast, Marco again crossed the great Yangtze River. Marco insisted the Yangtze was the mightiest river in the world. From west to east it flowed a twisting course through the entire Mongol Empire carrying trading ships. At the river city of Chen-Chou, Marco counted fifteen thousand vessels at one time. Teams of horses along the riverbank towed ships upstream by long ropes. A customs officer of the Great Khan told Marco that two hundred thousand vessels passed upstream each year.

Farther to the south Marco admired the city of Suchow (modern-day Suzhou), with its six thousand handsome stone bridges.

Above and opposite page: View of Kinsai, the "City of Heaven"; Chinese painting; early Ming dynasty, 14th-15th century; "Panorama of West Lake at Hang Chou"; color on paper makimono: 1657.3 x 32.7 cm (652 9/16 x 12 7/8 in.)

Riding onward, he soon entered an even more magnificent city. The name of the city of Kinsai (modern-day Hangzhou) meant "City of Heaven" in Chinese. "The city is beyond dispute the finest and the noblest in the world," Marco later boasted. Kinsai lay between a large lake and a great river. Canals cut gentle waterways between the lake and river, and twelve thousand high stone bridges connected the city's many separate islands. Perhaps Kinsai reminded Marco of Venice, but on a much grander scale.

In Kinsai stood 1,600,000 houses. St. Mark's Square was the single large marketplace in Venice. But Kinsai

possessed ten busy market squares, each a half-mile
(.8 kilometer) long and a half-mile wide. Twelve guilds,
or unions, of craftsmen each owned twelve thousand
shops where masters and apprentices worked at their
trades. A main avenue ran through the city from end
to end. "The crowd of people that you meet here at all
hours," declared Marco, "passing this way and that on
their different errands, is so vast that no one would
believe it possible." To feed so many people required
huge amounts of food. Marco noted, for example, that
the population spiced their meals with 10,000 pounds
(4,536 kilograms) of pepper each day.

The Chinese emperor of Manzi had fled Kinsai when the Mongols invaded his country. Marco visited his palace, however, and called it "the greatest palace in the world." Beautiful fruit trees and bubbling fountains filled the gardens outside. Inside, the walls and ceilings of twenty great halls and one thousand rooms dazzled the eye with fine drawings painted in gold.

Boating on the lake beside Kinsai offered pleasure on evenings and on days of rest. People sat in relaxing comfort in the open cabins of flat-bottomed barges, while crews poled them back and forth over the glassy water. "It is the great delight of the citizens," revealed Marco. Flowering trees, noble houses, and religious temples provided lovely views along the water's edge. In the middle of the lake rose two islands. On each island stood a large beautiful pavilion, richly furnished. "And when anyone of the citizens desired to hold a marriage feast, or to give any other entertainment," recalled Marco, "it used to be done at one of these palaces." In different rooms, as many as one hundred different wedding parties, banquets, and happy celebrations could occur at the same time.

Most of the houses in Kinsai were made of wood. Fire remained a constant danger. Therefore the city devised a fire-fighting system. Through all hours of the day, watchmen stood at every bridge holding wooden drums. "If they see that any house has caught fire they immediately beat upon that wooden instrument to give the alarm," Marco explained. At the sound of the drumbeat, watchmen from all of the nearby bridges came running to help douse the flames with water. Patrols of watchmen also walked the streets at night, making sure that all was quiet and lights and fires were out.

The people of Kinsai looked handsome in their silk clothes. In business they behaved with honesty, and in every neighborhood citizens looked out for one another. Everywhere Marco felt an atmosphere of peace and friendliness. City guards who found crippled beggars in the streets helped them to hospitals for care. Jobless men were led to craft shops and given employment. Springs provided water for some three thousand public baths in the city. "They are the finest and largest baths in the world," insisted Marco, "large enough for 100 persons to bathe together." Cheerfully Kinsai citizens soaked themselves clean in the hot bathhouse water several times a month.

Detail from Street Scenes in Times of Peace (Taiping fenghui tu), view #9: the Fortune Tellers; attributed to Zhu Junbi; Chinese handscroll, ink and color on paper, 26 x 790 cm; Ming Dynasty, 15th-16th centuries; The Art Institute of Chicago, Kate S. Buckingham Fund, 1952.8

An ancient watchtower and mile-stone along a highway in northern China

"All the streets of the city are paved with stone or brick," commented Marco, "as indeed are all the highways throughout Manzi." At last the time arrived for Marco to leave the wonderful "City of Heaven." With fond memories, he rode the paved highway back to Khanbalik.

It is unknown how many missions Marco Polo carried out in service to the Great Khan. Certainly, though, his many journeys gave him a greater knowledge of the world than anyone before. In their private quarters in the palace at Khanbalik, Marco told his father and uncle of the wonderful things he had seen. Nicolo and Maffeo showed Marco the bright gems they had acquired by trading. As the years slipped by, the three Venetians began to think more and more of home.

The Great Khan was growing older, and the Polos depended on his good will and protection. At court, some noblemen already regarded Marco's high position with jealousy. If the Great Khan died, the Polos guessed they would receive poor treatment afterwards. In addition, Nicolo and Maffeo could not wait much longer. Soon they would be too old to make the long and difficult journey westward.

Repeatedly the Polos presented the Great Khan with their respectful request to leave. But the emperor greatly enjoyed their company and depended on their loyal service. Nothing could persuade him to permit the Polos to go. Instead he offered them greater honors and rewards of treasure to stay. A full seventeen years passed, and the Polos expected to die in China. Then in 1291, the Polos grasped at a chance to get away at last.

Curved-roof structure in the Forbidden City, a walled section of Beijing where China's emperors used to live

Chapter 9
Princess Cocachin

By a twist of fate, the dying wish of a Persian queen gave the Polos their opportunity to leave Cathay. The ruler of Persia, Arghun Khan, deeply loved his favorite wife, Bolgana. In the year 1286, Queen Bolgana fell gravely ill. As doctors hopelessly attended her, Bolgana asked that her husband choose as his next wife a woman from her Mongol clan. After Bolgana died, Arghun Khan vowed to carry out her last wish. He selected three ambassadors and sent them overland to the court of his great-uncle Kublai Khan.

Sometime in the year 1288, the Persian ambassadors arrived at Khanbalik. Respectfully they asked that the Great Khan select a new bride for Arghun Khan from the women of Bolgana's Mongol clan. To fill Bolgana's place, the Great Khan chose a princess named Cocachin. "She was a maiden of seventeen," remembered Marco Polo, "a very beautiful and charming person." When Cocachin presented herself at court, the Persian ambassadors declared that they were very pleased with her.

With much fanfare the three Persians, Princess Cocachin, maids, servants, and honor guards started overland to Persia in a royal caravan. Weary months of travel along the desert route brought the party to the mountainous frontier of central Asia. Unexpected dangers on the road ahead prevented further progress. Rival Mongol bands were fighting for control of the region. For safety's sake, the Persian ambassadors decided to return to Cathay. After eight difficult months, Princess Cocachin's royal caravan returned through the gates of Khanbalik.

The Persian ambassadors reported to the Great Khan. Unhappily they wondered how to carry out their mission. By lucky chance, however, Marco Polo had just then returned from a long sea voyage to India. Marco had been sent there to obtain religious items for the Great Khan's sacred collection. At court the Persian ambassadors listened as Marco reported on his journey. Marco's knowledge of the sea route greatly impressed the three Persians. Perhaps with Marco's help they could travel to Persia by sea.

Secretly the Polos and the Persian ambassadors discussed the idea. Finally the three Persians begged the Great Khan for permission to travel by sea and to take the Polos with them as guides. The thought of losing the company of the Polos upset the Great Khan. However, he realized the importance of honoring Arghun Khan's wish. In order to transport princess Cocachin to Persia without further delay, he gave his consent.

The emperor called the Polos before him. He presented the Venetians with two tablets of gold. These tablets guaranteed them safe passage and assistance throughout the Mongol Empire. He gave them diplo-

The Polos' ships gathered at Zaiton

matic letters to carry to the pope and the kings of Europe. Gratefully the Polos also accepted gifts of sparkling rubies and other jewels. They had served the Great Khan faithfully for seventeen years. Now as the three Venetians bid the emperor goodbye, they pledged to carry out this final important mission for him.

The royal caravan journeyed the paved highways of Cathay and Manzi and in time reached the great Chinese seaport of Zaiton (present-day Xiamen). By order of the Great Khan, sea captains were preparing a fleet of thirteen ships for use on the expedition. Sailors carried aboard enough food and equipment to last two years.

Marco Polo remarked upon the sturdy quality of these ships. Thick hulls of double planking studded with nails protected these great four-masted vessels. Below deck the largest ships possessed as many as sixty cabins for passengers. Sailors stowed cargo in other large compartments. "The planking is so well fitted," marveled Marco, "that . . . water can not pass from one compartment to another." If a damaged hull leaked, the crew could empty the leaking compartment and repair it without fear of sinking. Shipbuilders in Europe did not use such a clever design of watertight compartments.

At last the Polos, along with Princess Cocachin and her bridal party, boarded the readied ships. On a spring day in 1292, the captains gave their orders and the sailors hoisted sails. The royal fleet coasted out among the waves of the South China Sea.

Across the vast ocean far to the northeast stood Cipangu (present-day Japan). Though he never visited Japan himself, Marco had heard many stories of that land. He included some of them in his description of the world. The people of Cipangu were civilized, explained Marco, and possessed great treasures of gold. "I will tell you a wonderful thing about the Palace of the ruler of that Island," Marco further declared. "You must know that he hath a great Palace which is entirely roofed with fine gold. . . . Moreover, all the . . . floors of its chambers are entirely of gold, in plates like slabs of stone . . . and the windows also are of gold, so that altogether the richness of this Palace is past all bounds and all belief."

In the year 1275, when the Polos first arrived in Cathay, Kublai Khan launched an invasion fleet to conquer Cipangu. That attempt failed, and he sent a second great fleet in 1281. The ships reached the defenseless Japanese coast just as disaster struck. "It came to pass," exclaimed Marco, "that there arose a north wind which blew with great fury. . . . It blew so hard that the Great Khan's fleet could not stand against it." The howling storm drove dozens of ships to wreck ashore. Thousands of men drowned beneath the waves. The Japanese were saved by this storm, and it became part of their national legend. They called it the *kamikaze*, the "Divine Wind."

For two months the Polos and Princess Cocachin sailed with their royal fleet across the South China Sea. "You must know," Marco later told, "that on leaving the port of Zaiton you sail west-south-west for 1,500 miles [2,414 kilometers], and then you come to a country called Champa" (present-day Vietnam).

"There are very great numbers of elephants in this kingdom," declared Marco. The jungles were rich with sweet-smelling aloe wood and forests of jet-black ebony. Though independent of the Mongol Empire, Champa remained under the Great Khan's influence. Marco revealed that the king of Champa respectfully sent the Great Khan a yearly gift of "20 of the greatest and finest elephants that were to be found in the country."

From Champa the sea voyage carried the travelers far to the south to the island of Java (part of present-day Indonesia). Hundreds of merchant ships gathered in the busy ports of Java. Black peppers, nutmegs, cloves, and other valued spices grew in abundance on Java and made the island the center of Asia's spice trade. To gain its wealth of spices, the Great Khan had often considered invading the island. But it lay too far from the mainland.

Sago palm

Orangutan

The royal fleet sailed calmly among lesser islands of Indonesia until caught by the sweeping rains of the monsoon season. Through five months of stormy weather, the ships took refuge along the coast of the great island of Sumatra. On shore the Polos pitched camp and ordered their sailors to dig ditches all around, build wooden towers, and post guards. They greatly feared an attack by Sumatra's cannibals. The natives they encountered, however, proved friendly and willing to trade food for trinkets.

On Sumatra Marco claimed he saw strange trees. "These trees," he insisted, "are very tall and thick, but have a very thin bark, and inside they are crammed with flour." It is known today that the core of the sago palm found in Sumatra is indeed filled with a powdery starch that can be baked into bread.

Marco noted that natives tapped another kind of tree and made wine from the dripping liquid. Surely this was the East Indian toddy palm tree, whose sap can be made into liquor. The palm trees also yielded nuts "as big as a man's head," exclaimed Marco. The white nut inside the shell tasted sweet and chewy, and the milky liquid found deeper within was, declared Marco, "more delicate than any other drink that ever existed." These nuts amazed Marco because Europeans had never seen coconuts before.

On Sumatra Marco heard of a mountain tribe of wild men with tails. He never saw any of these fabled creatures himself, and probably they were orangutans. During his stay on the island, Marco did see "unicorns" with his own eyes. Unlike the graceful, horselike unicorns of European legend, these unicorns were nearly the size of elephants. "They have hair like that of a buffalo," exclaimed Marco, "feet like

Marco Polo's "unicorn" was probably a rhinoceros

those of an elephant, and a horn in the middle of the forehead, which is black and very thick. . . . 'Tis a passing ugly beast to look upon, and is not in the least like that which our stories tell of." Clearly these animals were the species of rhinoceros still found in Sumatra.

At last the weather cleared. The royal ships raised anchors and continued on their way. Westward in the Indian Ocean, the fleet stopped at both the Nicobar and Andaman Islands. Marco noticed that the jungles of these islands offered spices and valuable hardwood trees. But the natives at that time lived wildly without even a king.

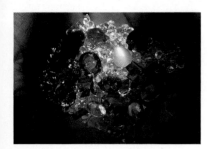

Semi-precious stones from the mines of Sri Lanka

A great open stretch of sea now lay before the fleet. Bravely the travelers pressed ahead in a westerly direction. "When you leave the Island of Andaman," explained Marco, "and sail about a thousand miles . . . you come to the Island of Ceylon." The dazzling gemstones found in Ceylon (modern-day Sri Lanka) greatly amazed Marco. Miners dug rubies, sapphires, topazes, and amethysts from the ground. "The King of this Island," declared Marco, "possesses a ruby which is the finest and biggest in the world." Marco insisted the stunning jewel was the size of a man's fist and "red as fire."

It was probably in Ceylon that Marco had obtained religious relics for the Great Khan during a mission in 1284. Buddhists believed the founder of their religion—Siddhartha Gautama, known as the Buddha—was buried on a Ceylon mountaintop. Muslims believed that the body buried there was that of the first man, Adam. During his mission Marco climbed the mountain and obtained teeth, hair, and an eating bowl at the sacred tomb. These he presented to a grateful Kublai Khan upon his return to Khanbalik.

Across a narrow gulf from Ceylon stood the southern coast of India. In April and May of every year, great fleets of Indian pearl fishermen eagerly sailed into the shallow waters of this gulf. When they reached the region where the pearl beds could be found, the ships dropped anchor. The pearl divers climbed into smaller boats and rowed out to work. "They jump into the water," observed Marco, "and dive to the bottom." At depths ranging from twenty to seventy feet (six to twenty-one meters), Marco further explained, "they find the shells that contain the pearls and these they put into a net bag tied round the waist. . . . When they

View from the top of the mountain called Adam's Peak in Sri Lanka

Pearl divers in the Indian Ocean

can't hold their breath any longer they come up again, and after a little down they go once more, and so they go on all day." On board their ships, the men cracked open the oyster shells and dug out any pearls they found inside. These waters provided pearls for the entire world market and kept the local Indian king in riches.

Sailing onward, the royal fleet stopped at ports along the Indian coast. The climate of southern India made a strong impression on Marco. "I assure you," he later declared, "that the heat of the sun is so great there that it is scarcely to be endured; in fact if you put an egg into one of the rivers it will be boiled, before you have had time to go any distance, by the mere heat of the sun!"

Brahman priests in a rural temple in northern India

The wide variety of animals found in southern India amazed Marco, too. "There are lions black all over, with no mixture of any other color." Perhaps he meant panthers. "And there are parrots of many sorts, for some are white as snow with red beak and feet, and some are red, and some are blue, forming the most charming sight in the world. . . . In short, everything they have is different from ours, and finer and better."

In this part of the world, many of the people followed the Hindu faith. The highest class of Hindus were called Brahmans, and they regarded the ox as a sacred animal. These Brahmans were completely honest people and very superstitious. They looked for

A devout Hindu praying on the banks of the Ganges River

lucky signs in everything. Such omens as a sneeze, a shadow on a wall, or the simple movement of a spider influenced their decisions.

Men of the deeply religious Hindu group called *yogis* often wore no clothes. Marco asked why they did so and was told, "We go naked because naked we came into the world, and we desire to have nothing about us that is of this world." By studying the yogis, Marco learned about the Hindu belief in the reincarnation of souls. "They would not kill an animal on any account," he remarked, "not even a fly, or a flea, or a louse, or anything in fact that has life; for they say these have all souls, and it would be sin to do so."

After leaving the coast of southern India, helmsmen on the royal ships steered again into the open sea. Off the coast of Africa lay the great island of Madagascar. According to stories Marco heard, a frightening beast called the griffin, or roc, lived in that region. This giant bird looked much like an eagle. "It is so strong," exclaimed Marco, "that it will seize an elephant in its talons and carry him high into the air, and drop him so that he is smashed to pieces." After killing an elephant by this method, the bird would swoop down and eat. The incredible legend of the roc is also recorded in the adventures of Sindbad the Sailor in *The Arabian Nights*.

Much more believable are the stories Marco told of Indian pirates. Sailing forth from coastal ports, Indian pirate ships gathered into fleets of twenty or thirty.

The roc, the legendary bird of the Indian Ocean area

Sailing forward in a row, each ship remained five or six miles (eight or ten kilometers) distant from the next. "They cover something like a hundred miles of sea," warned Marco, "and no merchant ship can escape them."

Perhaps one such fleet of pirates attacked the Polos' ships. Marco gives no details in his book, but the royal fleet surely endured many dangers during it sea voyage. Accidents, storms, and sickness claimed the lives of both passengers and crewmen. At the end of two long years, the royal fleet finally sailed into the Persian seaport of Hormuz. Six hundred passengers had left Zaiton in Princess Cocachin's bridal party, "but nearly all died by the way," Marco solemnly revealed. In fact, it is amazing to learn that only eight passengers survived the difficult trip, including Princess Cocachin, Nicolo, Maffeo, and Marco Polo.

The Polos landing in Hormuz on the Persian Gulf

Chapter 10
Marco Millions

Gladly the Polos escorted Princess Cocachin ashore at Hormuz. They believed the most important part of their mission was at an end. They needed only to bring Princess Cocachin to the Persian court for her wedding to Arghun Khan. Their smiles soon turned to frowns, however, when they learned that old Arghun Khan had died. They hardly knew what to do next. They could not abandon Princess Cocachin in a foreign land. Yet it seemed that their long, difficult journey no longer had a purpose.

In search of an answer, the Polos accompanied Princess Cocachin to the royal court. The death of Arghun Khan had left all of Persia in confusion. Arghun Khan's son and heir, Ghazan, was away on military duty protecting Persia's northern frontier. In his place, his uncle Kaikhatu was occupying the throne. The Polos rode across the familiar Persian countryside and arrived at the royal court. Respectfully the Venetian ambassadors reported to Kaikhatu and presented the Mongol princess.

Since Arghun Khan was dead, Kaikhatu wisely suggested that Princess Cocachin marry Prince Ghazan instead. Weeks of dusty travel along Persian caravan routes brought the travelers at last to the army encampment of Ghazan. The brave and noble Persian prince accepted the proposal and agreed to marry the lovely Cocachin. In time, the royal couple would rule Persia as king and queen.

Their royal mission completed, the Polos took their leave of Princess Cocachin. During the long journey from Cathay they had shared many adventures together. She trusted and admired the three Venetians. The Polos felt a deep fondness for her as well. With mixed emotions the three men mounted their horses, and Princess Cocachin wept with sorrow as they said good-bye.

Free to return home, the Polos stopped first at the court of Kaikhatu, probably at the Persian city of Tabriz. For several months they rested as guests of the Persian ruler. During that time, they learned that Kublai Khan had died. The death of the Great Khan saddened the Polos. But they knew they had made the right decision in leaving Cathay when they did. When at last the Polos prepared to leave Persia, Kaikhatu presented them with golden tablet passports and ordered a guard of two hundred horsemen to guide them safely on their way.

Warring armies of Muslims made direct travel to the Mediterranean seacoast impossible. Therefore the Polos chose a route that led farther to the north. "Having left Kaikhatu," Rustichello penned in *The Travels*, "they traveled day by day till they came to Trebizond." This Turkish city beside the Black Sea filled the Polos with excitement. Venetian merchants lived in houses along the broad avenues. In cheerful conversation, the Polos learned all the news from Venice. Powerful Greeks and Genoese living in Trebizond cheated the Polos of some of the wealth they had carried out of China. That bitter disappointment made Marco, Nicolo, and Maffeo long for home all the more. Boarding a ship, they sailed across the Black Sea to Constantinople. From Constantinople

Ships sailing into Venice

they next sailed into the Mediterranean. Around the tip of Greece the winds blew their ship until, at long last, sometime in the year 1295, a lookout shouted that the island city of Venice lay just ahead.

Soon the ship docked and the Polos climbed ashore. For the first time in twenty-five years, they walked the streets of Venice. Marco had left as a teenager and was returning a middle-aged man. As he stepped along, he must have felt as if he were awakening from a long, fantastic dream. Gondoliers steered their boats along the canals. Church bells called citizens to Mass. Merchants crowded together at the Rialto making deals. Here and there, work crews cleared the rubble of old buildings and stonemasons erected new ones. But altogether Venice had not changed very much. It was Marco Polo who had changed.

The Polos' servants and slaves carried packages and followed behind their masters. The group entered the San Giovanni Chrisostimo district of the city. Through gateways and courtyards they stepped until they reached the Polo house. There is no record of what happened next. Legend states that relatives now lived in the house as if it were their own. They answered a knock at the door and saw three strange men standing before them. The men looked weather-beaten and weary. They were dressed in coarse, worn clothes sewn in the style of the Mongols. After years in Asia, Marco, Nicolo, and Maffeo had nearly forgotten their native language. In thick accents they introduced themselves.

At first their relatives refused to believe them. These foreign-looking men in their ragged clothes seemed nothing at all like the three well-dressed merchants who had left Venice twenty-five years earlier. The wives of Nicolo and Maffeo stared at the two white-haired men but could not recognize their long-lost husbands. Others wondered aloud if the grown man standing in the doorway could possibly be young Marco.

Full of doubt, the family finally allowed the three strangers to walk inside. The men sat and ate and told stories of the past. These old memories of loved ones slowly persuaded some members of the family that Marco, Nicolo, and Maffeo had indeed returned home. The strange tales they told of their travels, however, met with looks of total disbelief. These storytellers claimed they had been guests at beautiful Asian palaces. They spoke of fine cities and rich treasures. Yet they sat there dressed in ragged clothes.

To prove that they were not liars or fakes, the three Polos organized a banquet. By invitation, all of their relatives curiously attended. At this feast, Marco, Nicolo, and Maffeo sat at the table dressed in handsome red robes of satin, silk, and damask cloth brought from Asia. At the end of the meal the three men stood. Roughly they threw off their costly robes and walked out of the room.

The guests all wondered at this strange behavior. They watched closely as the three men soon returned wearing the shabby clothes they had worn while traveling home. After quietly crossing the room the three suddenly seized knives from the table. They ripped open the seams and linings of their clothes. From these openings spilled out streams of rubies, diamonds, emeralds, and sapphires. The guests gasped and gaped as a fortune in precious gems piled upon the table. Before starting their journey home the Polos had carefully sewn many of the jewels they had earned in China into these clothes. With such startling evidence of wealth as this, their relatives could doubt them no longer.

Nicolo and Maffeo Polo found comfort in their return to Venice. They had spent their lives traveling the world. A few relaxed years of retirement seemed attractive to these two old men. It was Marco, still a vigorous man in his early forties, who found it difficult to adjust to life in Venice. Venice seemed unimportant compared with the great cities he had seen. How could Venice compare with the graceful beauty of Kinsai? How could the greatest house in Venice compare with the palaces of Shangtu and Khanbalik? He hardly knew his relatives. His closest friends were the ones he left behind in China. Life as a Venetian merchant would be very boring after his many years of worldwide adventure.

Marco told his stories of Asia to whoever would listen. He showed his visitors yak wool, the dried head of a musk deer, and a bag of flour from the amazing sago palm tree. He passed around the seeds of various Asian trees and plants, which he later tried unsuccessfully to grow in Venetian soil. For a time, the stories Marco told of Asia filled his relatives and neighbors with wonder. Gradually, however, they grew tired of his boasts. Everything in Asia was the biggest, the finest, the best, according to Marco. His listeners openly laughed at some of the impossible things that he insisted were true.

Venetians could not be bothered by Marco Polo and his fantastic tales. At that time, the city-state of Venice was locked in a long and ugly war with its hated rival Genoa. Fleets of the two realms often clashed in savage combat at sea.

Perhaps Marco yearned for excitement or praise, or perhaps he wished to help his city. Whatever the reason, before long he volunteered to fight. His wealth and experience earned him the rank of a gentleman commander of a Venetian galley ship.

Captain Marco Polo commanded his ship with skill and bravely steered it into battle. It is uncertain where and when he fought. Sometime between the years 1296 and 1298, however, he was captured by the enemy while fighting at sea. It is possible his ship took part in the Battle of Curzola on September 7, 1298. On that day, a Venetian fleet unsuccessfully attacked a fleet of Genoese galleys near the island of Curzola in the Adriatic Sea. Amid the wreckage of smashed and burning ships, the Genoese sailors shouted in triumph. As a result of the bloody battle, thousands of Venetian seamen surrendered and many ships were captured.

Marco Polo's warship in battle with the Genoese

The prisoners and captured galleys were towed to Genoa. By the fall of 1298, Marco Polo found himself sitting in a crowded cell in Genoa's Palace San Giorgio. This might have become a time of deep bitterness for Marco, except for a lucky twist of fate. Bored cellmates passed idle hours telling the stories of their lives. Soon Marco was invited to tell something of his life, too. Once he had started, his fellow prisoners refused to let him stop. Marco spun wonderful tales of the Holy Land and the desert roads leading into Asia. He described everything his listeners wished to learn about the dreaded Mongols: how they lived, for example, and how their armies fought. He filled their minds with fantastic images of the court of Kublai Khan and the exotic cities of Cathay and Manzi.

Amazed jailors quickly spread word of their storytelling prisoner. Soon, curious Genoese citizens entered the cell at the Palace San Giorgio to hear Marco Polo's daily entertainments. More important, a Pisan prisoner named Rustichello stepped forward with an unusual offer for Marco. As a skilled writer of romances, Rustichello understood the special value of Marco's stories. He wished to write them down, and Marco gladly agreed.

The Genoese jailors provided Rustichello with paper, pens, and ink. Marco sent to Venice for the notes he had made while traveling through the Mongol Empire. Soon the work of writing began. Each day Rustichello scratched his inky pens across the papers while Marco told of the people, customs, geography, and products of the many lands he had visited. He described Persia, China, India, and other countries Europeans had never seen and could hardly imagine. Rustichello titled the book a *Description of the World*, but it would become best known as *The Travels of Marco Polo*. In its pages Rustichello honestly wrote, "I can assure you there never was a single man before who learned so much and beheld so much as he did."

At last, in the spring of 1299, the two men finished their book. The journeys of Marco, Nicolo, and Maffeo Polo were as completely described as Marco would ever tell them. On the last page of the manuscript, Marco humbly instructed Rustichello to write: "I believe it was God's pleasure that we should get back in order that people might learn about the things that the world contains." That same spring, a truce ended the war between Genoa and Venice. Released from prison, Marco Polo said farewell to Rustichello and returned to Venice.

Frontispiece from the first printed edition of Marco Polo's book, 1477

With happy smiles, Marco's family welcomed him home again. After months of prison, Marco rested for a time. When he thought about his future, he realized it was time he had a wife. Before long he found a suitable young woman whose family agreed to the match. At the age of forty-five, Marco Polo married Donata Badoer. Ringing church bells and a joyful wedding feast marked the happy day. In the years that followed, the couple had three daughters: Fantina, Bellela, and Moreta.

Marco resumed his career as a Venice merchant. He organized trading ships to carry cargo. He traded in such products as Russian furs and English tin. From Venice he shipped bales of woven cloth and crates of polished mirrors and glass oil lamps to the southern coast of the Mediterranean. In Venice marketplaces, Marco sometimes bartered for spices, gold, and jewels. His routine life as a Venice merchant was dull next to the excitement of his past, however. Constantly he talked of Asia. His family and neighbors heard his stories a hundred times. The wealth of China numbered in the millions, Marco insisted again and again. Incredible profits could be earned trading in Cathay. Venetian businessmen turned and walked away whenever Marco Polo started in with another of his unbelievable boasts. Finally his reputation as a

Marco Polo as an older man

teller of tall tales earned him the nickname "Marco Millions," and the Polo house became commonly known as "Millions Court."

In Venice, Marco Polo grew gray and old. His father died around the year 1300. Several years later his Uncle Maffeo also died. Marco lost the dearest companions of his life. Because people refused to believe his stories, he sometimes quarreled with his neighbors. As he sat at home before his fireplace, perhaps he cursed those people who laughed at him and called him Marco Millions. Perhaps he closed his eyes and let his mind wander back on fabulous Asian journeys.

In the winter of 1323, Marco Polo's health began to fail. His wife and daughters kept a watch at his bedside, but he grew weaker every day. The family called in a physician who examined the old man and prescribed medicines. By January 8, 1324, however, it was clear that Marco Polo lay near death. Servants ran into the street to fetch a priest. The attending doctor also urged the family to hire a legal notary to write Marco's last will and testament. Soon a notary sat beside the bed with a ready pen. Slowly Marco Polo dictated his last wishes.

In his will the old traveler freed a faithful servant, his Mongol slave Pietro. He also divided his money and household furnishings, making sure that his wife and daughters received fair shares. Before long, this final work was done. The notary and three witnesses signed the document. Seventy-year-old Marco lay back upon his pillows. The priest stood nearby to administer the last rites. Sometime during that evening of January 8, Marco Polo breathed his final breath. The family buried him in the Church of San Lorenzo beside the body of his father.

Of the gifts that Marco Polo left behind, surely the book he wrote with Rustichello was the greatest. During Marco's lifetime *The Travels* became a medieval best-seller. Men who could write—monks, scribes, and scholars—made copies of the book by hand. Through the years it appeared in several European languages, including French, Spanish, German, and Irish. In European castles and manors, noblemen read the book with pleasure. But few people believed all the things they read. Marco Polo made claims that seemed simply impossible. His picture of the great wide world was more than Europeans could understand. So they read the book as if it were a wonderful fantasy.

Only with the passage of time did people realize how truthful Marco had been. Merchants and explorers who followed in his footsteps discovered the roads, climates, and cities just as Marco Polo had described them. By the 1400s, mapmakers used Marco's book to draw more complete maps of the world. European religious scholars used the text to learn about the Buddhist and Hindu faiths. Historians found the book useful in studies of the Mongol Empire. Marco's stories of the wealth of China and Japan filled one special explorer with dreams of riches. Using *The Travels* as one of his guides, Christopher Columbus set sail from Spain in the *Niña*, the *Pinta*, and the *Santa María* in 1492. Full of courage, Columbus hoped to reach Asia by sailing west across the Atlantic Ocean. Instead he discovered an entirely new world in the Western Hemisphere.

The Travels of Marco Polo is probably the most remarkable book of travels ever written. Few people have lived fuller lives, faced more dangers, or witnessed more beauty and splendor than did Marco Polo.

This keen-eyed merchant, dutiful ambassador, and fearless explorer lived and saw more than even he could tell.

According to legend, as Marco Polo lay in bed at the end of his life, the priest stepped forward and bent low beside him. He asked the dying man if he wished to take back some of the stories he had told. Surely he did not wish to die with any lies on his conscience. Instead the great explorer whispered in the priest's ear, "I did not tell half of what I saw, for I knew I would not be believed."

A European artist's conception of medieval China

Appendix

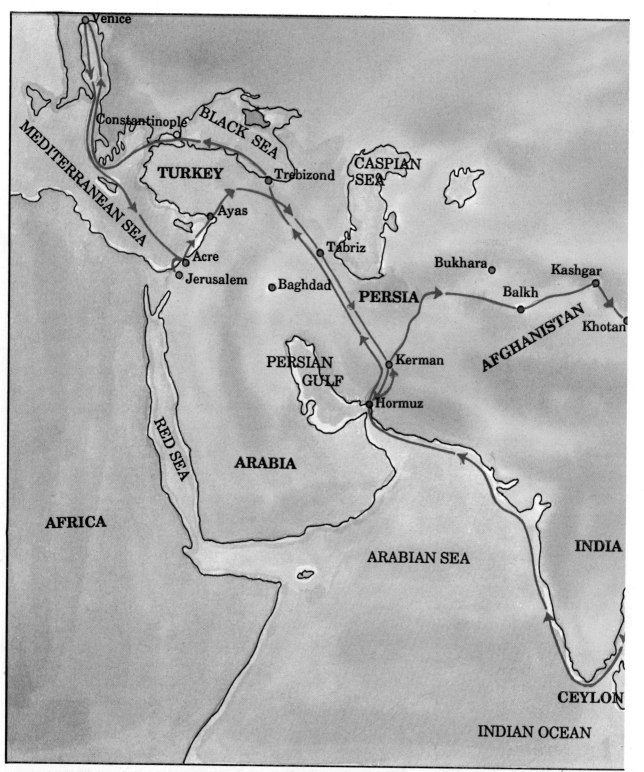

Route of Marco Polo's Travels

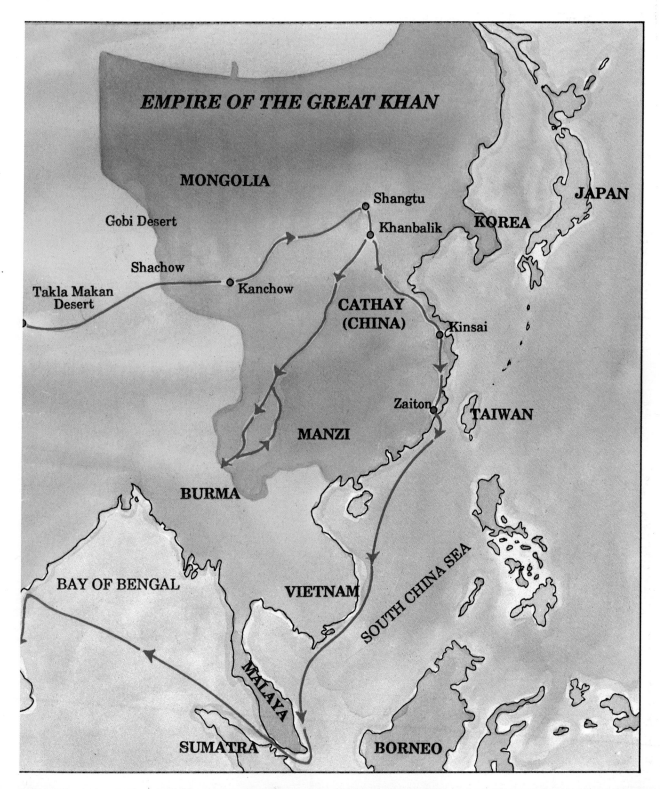

Timeline of Events in Marco Polo's Lifetime

1254—Marco Polo is born in the San Giovanni Chrisostimo district of Venice; his father Nicolo and uncle Maffeo head eastward on a trading venture, stopping for six years in Constantinople

1258—Mongol chief Hulagu Khan captures the city of Baghdad from the ruling caliph

1260—Nicolo and Maffeo leave Constantinople and travel to the Volga River region; Kublai Khan, grandson of Genghis Khan, becomes the emperor of the Mongol Empire

1262—The Polo brothers leave the Volga region and head farther east, hoping to find a roundabout way home; they stay in the Persian city of Bukhara for three years

1265—Ambassadors of Kublai Khan convince the Polo brothers to go with them to Cathay (China) and visit Kublai Khan

1266—The Polos leave Cathay, promising Kublai Khan that they will go on missions for him to the pope and to Jerusalem

1269—The Polo brothers return to Venice

1271—Nicolo, Maffeo, and Marco Polo embark on a journey to Cathay, stopping in Acre and Jerusalem on the way

1272—Mongol warriors begin their conquest of Burma

1275—After an arduous trip across the mountains and deserts of Asia, the Polos arrive at Kublai Khan's summer palace in Shangtu; Kublai Khan launches a fleet on an unsuccessful invasion of Cipangu (Japan)

1279—China's Song dynasty, with its capital in Kinsai, falls to Kublai Khan, who establishes the Yuan dynasty; Mongols now control all of China

1280s—At the request of Kublai Khan, Marco goes on several expeditions in the southern part of the empire

1281—A fierce wind, called a *kamikaze*, destroys Kublai Khan's second fleet to invade Japan

1288—Mongol princess Cocachin and her escorts begin a journey to Persia, where she is to marry the khan of Persia, but the travelers are turned back by warring hordes

1292—After seventeen years at the court of Kublai Khan, the Polos sail from China to escort Princess Cocachin to Persia

1295—The Polos reach Venice again

Between 1296 and 1298—Marco is captured in a sea battle between Venice and Genoa; he is imprisoned in Genoa's Palace San Giorgio

1299—Venice and Genoa reach a truce and Marco is released from jail; having dictated his adventures to the writer Rustichello, he leaves with the book, returns to Venice, and marries Donata Badoer; they eventually have three daughters

Around 1300—Marco's father, Nicolo, dies in Venice

1324—Marco Polo dies on January 8 in Venice

Glossary of Terms

ambassador—An official representative or messenger of a ruler

asbestos—A fireproof mineral that can be separated into long fibers and then woven

astrologer—Someone who studies the supposed effects of stars and planets on human affairs

bamboo—Tall, woody grasses with hollow, segmented stems

caliph—Up through the 1300s, a Muslim leader who was considered to be a successor of Muhammad, founder of the Islamic faith

cannibal—A creature that eats members of its own species

caravan—A long string of travelers with wagons or pack animals

cavalcade—A procession, usually with people on horseback or in carriages or other vehicles

cheetah—A spotted, swift-running member of the cat family; found in Africa and formerly also in Asia

clogs—Shoes with thick wooden soles

continent—One of the seven great land masses on earth

courtier—An attendant at a king's or queen's court

Crusades—Christian military campaigns taken in the eleventh through thirteenth centuries to retake the Holy Land from Muslims

curfew—A rule requiring people to be home, or at least off the streets, by a certain time at night

diplomatic—Having to do with relations between rulers or nations

ebony—A hard, black wood that comes from the ebony tree

fanfare—A grand and glorious display

felt—A fuzzy fabric made of tightly woven wool or cotton

ford—Shallow part of a river where people can wade across

friar—Member of a religious order devoted to prayer and preaching

frontier—The border or the farthest limits of a country or territory

galley—A large Mediterranean sailing ship used for trade and battle

gilt—Covered with gold or with something that looks like gold

gondola—A long, narrow boat such as those used to travel on Venice's canals

gondolier—A boatman who steers a gondola using a long pole

haphazard—Random; having no plan or direction

hoard—To store up a hidden supply of something

horde—A tribe of nomadic Mongols; any large group or crowd; from the Mongolian word *orda*, meaning "camp"

Islam—A religion founded by Muhammad in the seventh century

ivory—The hard, white tusk material of elephants or walruses

kamikaze—A Japanese airplane pilot in World War II who was to make suicidal crashes on ships or other targets; the Japanese word means "divine wind"

khan—A medieval Chinese ruler; a chief in some central Asian countries

kumiss—A drink made of fermented mare's milk

lacquered—Coated with a shiny varnish

lustrous—Glittering, sparkling, shiny

manuscript—A typed or handwritten copy of a book or story

medieval—Relating to the Middle Ages, a period in European history lasting from about A.D. 500 to 1500

merchandise—Goods that are bought and sold

monsoon—A heavy wind or rain storm that takes place during certain seasons in southern Asia

mosaic—An artistic picture or pattern formed by small bits of colored material

musk—A substance produced by the male musk deer of central Asia and used in making perfumes

Muslim—A follower of the religion of Islam

nomads—People with no permanent residence who move from place to place with the seasons to find food

orangutan—A tree-dwelling ape of Borneo and Sumatra

pageant—A dazzling program of music, drama, and processions

parchment—Sheepskin or goatskin prepared so it can be written upon

pavilion—A large tent, canopy, or other shelter

plateau—A high, flat stretch of land

retinue—A group of servants and attendants

scholar—A person who has studied a certain subject extensively

shah—A ruler of Persia (Iran)

sheik—The chief of an Arab clan, tribe, or country

sorcerer—A wizard; a magician who calls on the powers of evil spirits

steppes—Vast, treeless plains of Asia and eastern Europe

strait—A narrow channel of water between two bodies of land

truce—An agreement to stop fighting

unicorn—A mythical one-horned, horselike animal

Venetian—Having to do with Venice, Italy

vermilion—A bright red color

vizier—A high officer of an Islamic nation, especially of the old Turkish Empire

wharf—A structure on shore where ships can dock

yak—A long-haired ox that lives in mountainous regions of central Asia

yurt—A hide- or felt-covered tent of nomadic Mongols

zebu—An Asian ox that has a large hump on its back

Bibliography

For further reading, see:

Ceserani, Gian P. *Marco Polo*. NY: Putnam, 1982. (For younger readers)

Hart, Henry H. *Marco Polo: Venetian Adventurer*. Norman: University of Oklahoma Press, 1967.

Humble, Richard. *Marco Polo*. NY: Putnam, 1975.

Latham, Ronald, translator. *The Travels of Marco Polo*. London: Penguin Books, 1958.

Rugoff, Milton, and the editors of Horizon Magazine. *Marco Polo's Adventures in China*. NY: American Heritage Publishing Co., 1964.

Severin, Tim. *Tracking Marco Polo*. New York: Peter Bedrick Books, 1986. (For older readers)

Yule, Henry, editor and translator. *The Book of Ser Marco Polo*. NY: AMS Press, 1974. Reprint of 1903 edition.

Index

Page numbers in boldface type indicate illustrations.

Picture Identifications for Chapter Opening Spreads

6-7—St. Mark's Cathedral in Venice

14-15—Section of the Great Wall of China seen near Beijing

26-27—The Polos rowing into a port on the Black Sea, from a fourteenth-century manuscript

36-37—Sand dune desert in Uzbekistan, along the caravan route known as the Great Silk Road

48-49—Travelers across the Gobi Desert

56-57—Marco Polo welcomed at the court of Kublai Khan

72-73—Silkworm cocoons, from whose fibers silk cloth is woven

82-83—Life-size terra cotta warriors in the tomb of Emperor Shih Huang-ti (200s BC), who unified China and started building the Great Wall; near Xi'an

92-93—A sailing vessel at sunset off the coast of Cochin, India

106-107—Genoa, Italy, where Marco Polo was imprisoned

Acknowledgment

For a critical reading of the manuscript, our thanks to John Parker, Ph.D., Curator Emeritus, James Ford Bell Library, University of Minnesota, Minneapolis, Minnesota.

Picture Acknowledgments

About the Author

Zachary Kent grew up in Little Falls, New Jersey, and received an English degree from St. Lawrence University. After college he worked at a New York City literary agency for two years before launching his writing career. To support himself while writing, he has worked as a taxi driver, a shipping clerk, and a house painter. Mr. Kent has had a lifelong interest in history, especially American history. Studying the U.S. presidents was his childhood hobby. His collection of presidential items includes books, pictures, and games, as well as several autographed letters.